AF480380

ૐ
श्री गणेशाय नम :
श्री सरस्वत्यै नम :
ॐ भुर्भुव: स्व: तत्स वितुर्वरेिण्यम भर्गोदिवस्य धीमहीधियो यो न : प्रचोदयात्॥

# ETERNAL AND

# INCREDIBLE  INDIA

## COMPILATION OF QUOTATIONS IN PRAISE
## AND ON GLORY OF INDIA

## COMPILATION BY

## SHAILESH ANANTRAI TRIVEDI

© (2024) SHAILESH ANANTRAI TRIVEDI
Cover page and  illustrations :: NIRUPAMA TANK
MOGA
( Email :: niruart13@gmail.com)

# ETERNAL AND

# INCREDIBLE   INDIA

* * *

"In thought faith, In word wisdom,
In deed courage, In life service
So may India be great."

* * *

"विचार मेंविश्वास, शब्द मेंज्ञान ,

कर्म मेंसाहस, जीवन मेंसेवा ,

इसी रीति से - भारत महान हो।"

**INDIA IN ITS ESSENCE  IS …**

**ETERNALINDIA**

**INCREDIBLE INDIA**

**GLORIOUSINDIA**

**MAGINFICENTINDIA**

**GREATINDIA**

**DIVINEINDIA**

भारत अपने मूल-तत्व में हैं

शाश्वतभारत

अतुल्यभारत

यशस्वीभारत

भव्यभारत

महानभारत :: श्रेष्ठ भारत

दिव्य भारत

# THE WORK IS DEDICATED TO

ॐ

श्री गणेशाय नम :

श्री   सरस्वत्यै नमः

ॐ भूर्भुवः स्वःतत्सवितुर्वरेण्यंभर्गो देवस्यः धीमहिधियो यो नःप्रचोदयात् ॥

# :: THE WORK IS DEDICATED TO ::

## AT THE LOTUS FEET OF

## SHRI RAMKRISHNA PARAMAHANSA

## AND HIS DISCIPLE

## SWAMI VIVEKANANDA

## WHO HAS SEEN A DREAM FOR AWAKENED INDIA

At Kanyakumari, he decided to dedicate his life to the welfare and uplifting of the common masses of India.उत्तिष्ठ–जागृत-भारतARISE-AWAKE-BHARAT

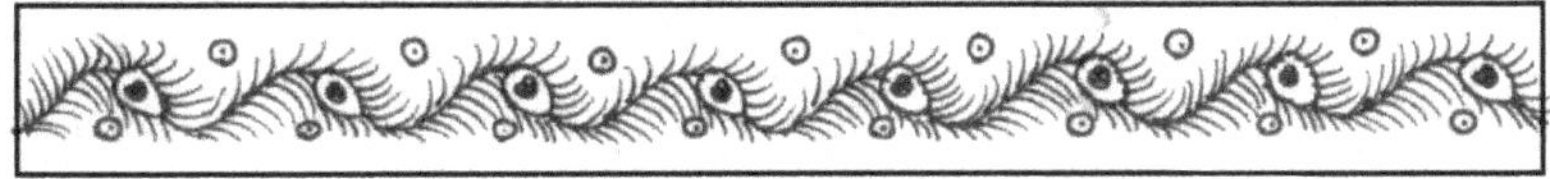

# PREFACE

The present work is about compilation and presenting in some categorical  order, of several inspiring, informative,  literary,  poetic  and  knowledgeable quotations aboutour Motherland India, by the various saints,  scholars, linguists, poets and philosophers through ages and from all over the world. It is a Simple, small and humble effort to get inspiration, increase awareness and to praise the glory and importance of our Motherland India that is Bharat-a nation and a civilization. It is further intended to introduce India's contribution to the world for the common cause and progress of human civilization and to the world in general. It is  the  wish and hope of the author  that the present work will be helpful in recognizing what it has intended, as mentioned above – to the students, young minds, teachers and all those who love, praise and respect India as a nation and her traditions,  customs, culture, civilization and  religion.

It is not claimed here that- the present work  is of compilation of several quotation on the  concept of nation and glory of India is a scholarly and research work. It is simply a compilation -and presented in the proper order as presented in this work. It is further not claimed that it is highly authentic and derived from its original sources. Most of  the content compiled  here is based on either secondary or  internet sources rather than, pure historical primary and original sources. It is still compiled – not for the purpose of -  to be referred for any scholarly or research work –but in order that reader may get inspired and benefited by this compilation-  to love respect and get themselves aware about the importance and glory of our  beloved Motherland India- an eternal Nation – revered and respected  by us all as Bharat Mata. This compilation is intended for all in whose heart the love and respect  of  India  is  lying  –  but  in  lack  of  proper information, they are not able to recognize how India is Eternal, Incredible, Magnificent, Great and Divine.

It is further to mention that the selection of the content, order in which it is presented, the part of the full content selected is neither perfect, complete and based on any standard or on any  rationale. This compilation is purely-  according to authors limited understanding, perception and  knowledge – it is purely compiled on the bases of the message of the content –found inspiring, encouraging and enlightening to the author- in order to respect our beloved nation- India that is Bharat. and so it is assumed that it will have similar effects in the heart of readers – having similar love, respect and admiration for the nation.

The content presented here is purely a compilation of quotation- about what a culture,nation,civilization and religion is and how it comes in to existence and what are the essence of all of them.These quotations are compiled from the write-ups from the writings of great saints, leaders, scholars, philosophers and laureates from India and across the globe. Once you go through this quotations you will realize that how the multidimensional, colorful, diverse, with full of variety,  ageless and  universal appeal of India's - cultural, national, civilization  and religious traditions,  has drawn attention and admiration, of scholars and philosophers, from all over the world, having background and upbringing indifferent language, culture, nation  and religion traditions.

The author is deeply indebted- and thankful to the authors, compilers, editors, publishers, web developers —whose literature is referred in the present work. Further author is also deeply indebted and thankful tothe  authors and publishers of,  several content which were  compiled directly from internet or some other reference material -  and it couldn't be recorded — and not possible to include in  references and hence  not included in reference and in acknowledgement. If anything found worthy or admirable by the reader in the present work —as it is only compilation and not any original work — the credit of that appreciation or admiration is lying absolutely -with all those who- are the original authors and   compilers-who have worked hard- either to create or to compile it fromits  primary sources. It is possible that all those to whom the real credit lies - may have name or may not have name, they may have been referred or may not have been refereed, they may be known or anonymous. And no such credit is claimed here by the author for the present work.It is only an humble and small effort to just introduce briefly the reader – about how really India is- an eternal and Incredible nation – above all an ageless civilization.

Acknowledgement is made here with   deep sense of gratitude- and with humble feeling of thanks – towards all the authors-compilers- web site developers,   whose work is referred here in the present work. A detail Acknowledgement is also included in present work for the authors of reference material –on the bases of that- this work is compiled.

Further it is not claimed that the present work is perfect, complete and full. Compilation is purely on the bases -of authors limited study, knowledge   and understanding capacity. It is possible that inspite ofproper  care taken, mistakes or errors may still be there in the work. Author is deeply regretting such mistakes and error. I humbly   beg  and request for  forgiveness and  Pardon to me,  for my any such  mistakes and error.

It is appealed to the reader to go through the content -simply in order to get awareness -and also insearch of inspiration, appreciation and admiration for our beloved motherland India –Bharat Mata. Reader is further cautioned about not to refer any content of the present work for any research or scholarly work – without thoroughly verifying it from its original or  primary source.

I am very much thankful  for artwork for the cover page and several other illustrations and designs of the book . to Ms. Nirupama Tank Moga ( <u>Email-niruart13@gmail.com</u>)

I am thankful to publishing platform Notion Press , Amazon, flipkart  and all other publishers who have helped me in publishing the present work, I am thankful to all my grandparents, parents, family members, relatives, friends, respected teachers, fellow studentsduring my  study at school and college, fellow professors, colleagues, students, neighbors. I am also thankful to all those who are with name or without name whose cooperation, blessings and well wishes has inspired me and has given courage and capacity  to compile and write this book- and made this work possible.

SHAILESH ANANTRAI TRIVEDI

"सनातन पथिक "    "SANATAN PATHIK"

Associate Professor
Civil Engineering

Vishwakarma Government Engineering College
Chandkheda-Ahmedabad-382424
Gujarat-India
Email -::- trivedisa12345@gmail.com

# THE ACKNOWLEDGEMENTS

Author is deeply indebted and highly thankful to all the authors, compilers, publishers  and web site developers  of  the primary source as being referred in the present work of compilation. The present work is only a compilation and collection and real credit rest with only original creators or compilers  with deep feelings of thanks they all are duly acknowledged hereby.  The details of the such original authors and reference is also mentioned in reference list of the present work – they all are duly acknowledged.

With deep feeling of thanks -Acknowledgment also to all those  authors  either mentioned or not mentioned, with name or without name whose work is referred in present work.

I humbly show my gratitude's and acknowledge their original  work,which has become a source of inspiration for the present compilation.

Further all the real credits are acknowledged to the authors, compilers, editors, publishers, website developers —whose literature is referred in the present work.

The author is deeply indebted and thankful to the authors, compilers, editors, publishers, web developers – whose literature is referred in the present work. Further author is also deeply indebted and thankful to authors and publishers of, several materials which were compiled directly from internet or some other reference material - and it couldn't be recorded – and not possible to include in references and hence not included in reference.

Author is thankful to all authors , publishers and creators and web site developers whose work is primarily referred in the present work. Acknowledgements to principle-internet website developers which has become major reference source of present work.

(1) https://www.wikipedia.org/

(2) https://en.wikiquote.org/wiki/Main_Page

(3) https://www.brainyquote.com/

(4) https://www.goodreads.com/quotes

(5) https://www.azquotes.com/

Special acknowledgements is mentioned below-
for some specific articles and content.

The reference source  of the some of the  part of
"Ancient Vedic Prayers" is deeply acknowledged - the
source of some  prayers  is article of Dr. Ravindra Kumar
" Nationalism in Vedas " published on Monday 8 th
August 2022, in Business Economics .

The reference source  of the  article 1.11  is deeply
acknowledged - the source of article 1.11 is Booklet "
Inscriptions in Parliament House " Published by
LoksabhaSecretriate, New Delhi May 2014.

The reference source  of the  of article 1.13  is
deeply acknowledged - the source of  part of Article 1.13
is  article of Josua J. Mark  " The Edicts of Ashoka the
Great  " published on Monday 29 th June  2020, in the
World History Organisation.

The reference source  of the  article 1.14  is deeply
acknowledged - the source of  Article 1.14 is  article of
Sidharth Bhatia   " India discovers herself again " The
full text of jawaharlal Nehru's " Tryst with destiny
speech   " published on 28 th August 2022 , in the Janta
Weekly.

With deep feelings of thanks —Acknowledgments
and attributes to original producers Wikipaedia.org and
Wikimedia- commons for the  several Images reproduced
in the present work for the purpose of  information,
awareness and respect for our nation. The detail
attributes are mentioned along with Image of Bharat
Mata, Swami Vivekanand,  Indian National Flag, Indian

National   Emblem,Indian   National   Currancy,   Indian
cockade    and Indian Sengol,where they appear in the
work.

# CONTENT

# INDIA IS BHARAT MATA

( (1) Attributes of the Image The Image reproduced here for information ,awareness and  in respect to Bharat Mata :: Originally created by -Akhand Hind Fauj – Licence Attribution Share Alike 4.0 International ( CC BY-SA 4.0),
(2) Web Site :: https://en.wikipedia.org/wiki/Bharat_Mata,
(3)Image Link ::
https://commons.wikimedia.org/wiki/File:Bharat-mata.png#/media/File:Bharat-mata.png
(4)Original Author Attribute link : By Akhand hind fauj - Own work, CC BY-SA 4.0,
(5)Liccence -CC BY-SA 4.0, Link ::
https://creativecommons.org/licenses/by-sa/4.0/)

## :: INDIA IS BHARAT MATA ::

India is not merely a geopolitical boundary, hence it is not only a country, but in its essence it is something more than that;

India is not merely about the customs, values, traditions and art hence it is not only a culture, but in its essence it is something more than that;

India is not merely aggregation of people of common descent, history, language and state hence it is not only a nation, but in its essence it is something more than that;

India is not merely about people who have attained very advanced level of culture, art , commerce and governance of state hence it is not only civilization, but in its essence it is something more than that;

India is not merely about people who have a particular system of faith, belief, and worship hence it is not only a religion, but in its essence, it is something more than that;

India is an eternal, ever-transforming, and reforming humane quest, for the spiritual interpretation of life, nature, soul, ultimate truth, and God ...

India is eternal as its history is unfathomable and her  culture has flown and existed in all ages and epochs. India's religious andcultural traditions  has remain uninterrupted and continuous throughout several millennia. While many other civilizations vanished, India still has preserved her antiquity till our times intake. It is a real sign of being eternal India.

India is incredible as her universal, diverse, multidimensional,multilingual,multireligious, multicultural,literary,social,architectural,  artistic,and  - all-pervading way of life- remain a source of inspiration throughout the globe. India's vast, wide, diverse, and multidimensional way of living makes her truly Incredible. Beyond anybody's capacity to be compared with or matched with.

India is Glorious as her  glory is spread across the globe since time antiquity. India was the supplier to the world  -of spices and precious tread commodities throughout history. India was abundant in such precious things so it can supply the entire globe.India's great warrior's sheds their bloods in brave wars. Mighty conquerors of the world find fierce resistance on this soil. India  has shown outstanding zeal in bravery. Her intellectuals created great literary epics and poetry. India invented great numerical system by introducing zero.Her industrious inhabitants produced-architectural monuments with amazing stone carving- tremendous wealth and gold-gewellerythroughout the centuries. It all makes India -a truly great nation.

India is Magnificent as the- land is blessed by God- like heaven. Her snowclad high mountains,roaring rivers, fertile planes, dense forest full of variety of species, flora and fauna. People with colorful and musical culture, beautiful and colorful clothing's full of embroidery. Marvelous stone architecture, shining gold and diamond ornaments, rich traditions and rituals, most melodious and meaningful prayers. Heavenly music and singing ,costume drama, delicious dishes in plentiful variety,her joyous and colorful festivals in tune with season and nature-all this truly make India a magnificent country.

India is rich in its diversity in religion, culture, literature, custom, traditions, rituals, worship styles and living styles. India has shown a fighting spirit to protect her rich culture and civilization. Brave warriors of India shed their blood in fight against invaders to protect her identity, civilization, religion and culture. India has not shown aspirations to catch others territory and wealth throughout the ages. India has always inspired seeking minds of the world through spreading her rich knowledge in language, mathematics, literature and science — all this make India a great country.

India is a land of seekers of knowledge-throughout her eternal existence. The greatest problems of existence of human life is sought on the high Himalayan mountains and on the shores of Indus,

Ganges, Godavari, Kaveri - like great rivers of India. India's religious traditions are so universal, diverse,  and total that it is  encompassing all the religious traditions of the entire world- combined together. The highest spiritual languages and   literature has flourished in India. The most beautiful and melodious prayers for God are being practiced in India since time antiquity. Anybody who is a seeker of spirituality his final refuge is often India -as India is citadel of humane spirituality. Making India truly a divine land .

India is the mother Goddess, Bharat Mata ...Ever caring and nourishing Mother ... Bharat mata  ki  Jai ...VandeMataram .. Jai Hind .

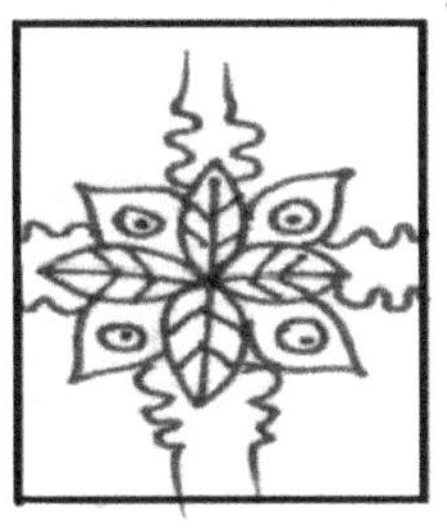

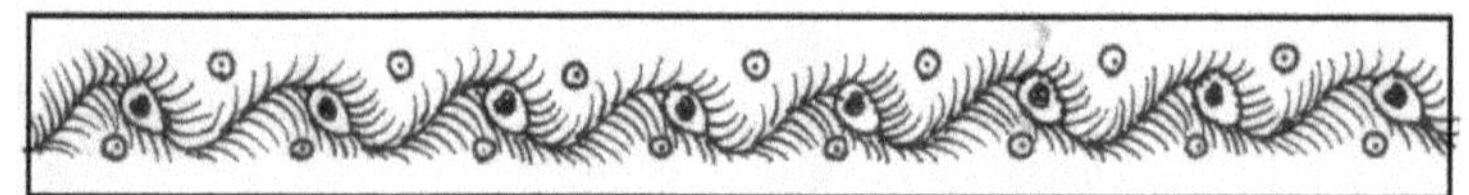

# PAYING RESPECT HOMAGE AND TRIBUTE TO GREAT SONS OF SOIL ...

**With deep feelings of thanks and bowing down our head in deep respect, we remember and  pay homage and tribute to ...**

All theKings -Warriors since ancient times who fought and laid their lives for libertysovereignty and independence. And for the protection of Indian civilization culture and religion.

All the Martyrs and Freedom Fighters who have sacrificed their property,family  and life for the struggle of independence.

All the Soldiers of the IndianArmy ,Navy and Air Force , Paramilitary forces  of our Indian nation who have sacrificed their  lives, and have sheds their blood for the protecting borders of India.

All the Preachers, Saints, Poets, Laureates, Philanthropists, Charity Workers,Social Reformers, and

Social Workersof our nation who preserved our culture and civilization.

All the erstwhile Maharajas, Former Rulers and Leaders of our great nation who led the nation with their hard work and enduring efforts.

All the recpients of Bharat Ratna, Padma Vibhushan, Padma Bhushan , Padma Shri,

All the recepients of Awards and Decorations of Indian Armed Forces- Param Vir Chakra, Mahavir Chakra, Vir Chakra , Ashok Chakra, Kirti Chakra , Shaurya Chakra, Sarvottam Yudh Seva Medal, Uttam Yudh Seva medal , Yudh Seva Medal, Param Vishisht Seva Medal, Ati Vishshisht Seva Medal, Vishisht Seva Medal, Sena Medal, Nau Sena Medal, Vayu Sena Medal, All Service and Campaign Medals, All Long Service Awards, All Independence Medals.

All the recpients of Sports Awards, Major Dhyan Chand Khel Ratna Award, Arjuna Award, Dronacharya Award, Major Dhyan Chand Award, Maulana Abul Kalam Azad Rolling Trophy, Rashtriy Khel Protsahan Purskar.

All recepients of Sahitya Academy Awards, Jnanpith Awards, Bhasha Samman, Awards for Translation, Yuva Puraskar , Golden Jubilee Awards.

All recpients of the Lalitkala Academy Awards in Music, Painting, Singing, Sculpture Performing Arts, Drama, National Film Awards, Dada Saheb Phalke Award.


All the Farmers, Doctors, Professors, Teachers, Authors, Scientists, Judges, Engineers, Lawyers, Police Personals,Journalists, Press Personals, Fire Fighters,Nursing and Paramedical staff, Pharmacists, Artists, Actors, Singers, Musicians, Dramatists, Painters, Sculputors, Sportsman, Political Leaders, OfficeBearers, Government Servants, Industrialists, Architects,Builders, Contractors, Suppliers, Sales-Persons, Caterers, Chefs, Chartered Accountants, Account personals, Businessman, Shop Owners, Merchants, Hawkers, Workers,Artisans, Gold Smiths, Jewellers, Pilots, Drivers, Sea Sailors, Fisherman,Skilled and Unskilled Laborers, Masons, Carpetners,Black Smith, Mechanic, Electrician,Workers,working in Agriculture Fields, Construction, Industries and in Sanitation and Cleanliness Works. And All Such Professionals AndWorkers of our nation who worked hard and shed their sweat to build our nation culture and civilization.


And above All-All the humble, kind and hard working silent citizens,from all religions, class, cast, creed, race, ethnicity any other background and with name or without name, known or unknown,who work hard and remained anonymous- their sacrifice for the cause of service to our nation, ultimately have build our culture, nation and civilization.

Our respect homage, and tribute to all beloved sons of soil , sons of Bharat Mata ....

There is a whole galaxy of great sons of our motherland India-Bharat mata. To name them all is a mammoth task and beyond any body's capacity. We respect them all. We respect the sacrifice of all of them. However as a mark of respect to all, mentioning in honor few- who were  equal among them.Weremember, respect, honor and salute to the sacrifice made by them for our nation. The names mentioned here represent also the names which are not mentioned here. It is representative of all great sons of our soil with name or without name.....

The Great Religious Preachers..

Lord Buddha, Lord Mahavira, Guru Nanak, Guru Arjundev,Shankaracharya,Ramanujacharya, Madhvacharya,                         Nimbarkacharya, Thiruvalluvaram,Nagarjuna,   MakhaaliGoshal,   Lord Swaminarayan, Ram Dev Pir, Osho, J. Krishnamurti .

The Great Saints..

Ramanand, Kabir, Ravidas,Raidas, Chaitnya, Mirabai, Tulsidas, Maharshi DayanandSarswati, Tukaram, Gyaneshwar, Namdev, Farid, RamkrishnaParamhans, Swami Vivekananda, Maharshi Arvind. A. C. Bhaktivedant swami Prabhupad, Raman Maharshi, Sai Baba, Satya Sai Baba, Amma, Sadguru, Prajapita Brahma, Dada Bhagwan, Maharshi Mahesh Yogi, Param Hans Yoganand, Maa Anandmayi ma, Devraha Baba, NimKaroli Baba, Shri Ram Sharma Avharya,Muni Tarun Sagar Maharaj, Sri Sri Ravishankar.

The Great Warrior Kings..

Porus,Dahir, ChandraguptMaurya, Bindusara, Ashoka the great,Akbar, Vikramaditya, Kanishka, Samudragupt,Pulkeshin, HemchandraVikramaditya, Raj Raja, Rajendra Chola, Bindusara, AjatShatru, Bimbisara, Raja Bhoj, Malavpati Munj, Krishndev Rai, Harshvardhan, PrithvirajChhauhan,Maharana Pratap, Chaatrapti Shivaji Maharaj,PadshahzadaDara Shikoh,Peshwa Bajirao, Maharaja Ranjitsingh, Rana Sanga, Raja Suheldev, Raja SurajmalJat, Bhimdev, SiddhrajJaisinh,Bapa Rawal, Rana Kumbha.

The Great Martyrs of India..

Guru Arjundev, Guru Tegbahadur, Sambhaji Maharaj, Gora-Badal,HamirSinhjiGohil,Bhai matidas,

Bhai Sati das, Banda singh Bahadur, Hari singh Nalwa,JhalaMansingh.

The Great  Freedom Struggle  Martyrs..

Mangal    Pandey,     MaharaniLaxmibai    of Jhansi,Tantya Tope,    Bhagat singh, Shivram Hari Rajguru, Sukhdev  Thapar, Ashfakulla Khan, Chandra shekhar   Azad,   Khudiram   Bose,   MatanginiHazra, Madanlal  Dhingra,  KartarsinghSarabha. Ram Prasad Bismil

The Great Freedom Fighters who were sent to Kalapani   Punishment   at   cellular   jail   Andaman ..Approximately 585 Freedom  Fighters  were  sent  to kalapaniduring freedom struggle few of them ..

Veer Savarkar, Diwan Sing kalepani, Yogendra Shukla, BatukeshwarDutt, Shadan Chandra Chattrjee, Sohan Singh, hare Krishna Konar, Shiv Verma, Allama Fazal –e-HaqKhairabadi, Sudhansu Dasgupta, Babarao Savarkar, Sachindranath Sanyal, Bhai parmanandSohan Singh   ,   Subodh   Roy,   TrailokyanathChakravarti, Barindra Kumar ghosh, Sher Ali Afridi, Mahavir Singh, Mohan  Kishore  namdas,  Mohit  Moitra,  Ulaskardutt, Barin Ghosh, Bhushan Roy, Chattar Singh, Baba Bhan Singh, Ram Raksha, Haripada Chowdhury , Dhirendra Chowdhury , Naringun Singh, Mehtab, Choitun, Mohan Kishore, Narain, ..

The Veterans of Azad Hind Fauz..

Netaji Subhash Chandra Bose, Maj. Gen Jaganth Rao Bhonsle, Col. Mohammad Zaman Kiani , Col. Shahnawaz Khan ,Col. G. S. Dhillon, Col .P. K. Sahgal, Capt. Lakshmi Sahgal, Capt. Abid Hasan, Capt, DilipsinghSiwach, Lt. R. H. Rizvi, Badriprasad Goswami, IndersingWarana

The Great Freedom Fighters..

Bahadur Shah Zafar, Begam hazarat Mahal, Nana sahib Peshwa, Kunwar Singh, Vinayak DamodarSavarkar, Birsa Munda, Bal Gangadhar Tilak, Lala Lajpat Rai, Bipinchandra Pal,ChakravartiRajgopalacharya, Rajendraprasad, Gopal krishanGokhale, Morarji Desai, Shyamji Krishn Verma, Aruna Yusuf Ali, PritilataWaddededar, Jatindranath Das, JatindranathMukharjee.

The Great Political Leaders..

Many of Them were also Great Freedom Fighters too..

Mahatma Gandhi, SardarVallabhbhai Patel, Jawaharlal Nehru, Subhashchandra Bose, Dr. B. R. Ambedkar, Lal Bahadur Shastri, Indira Gandhi, Atal Bihari Bajpai, Morarji Desai, Narendra Modi, Ram Manohar Lohia, Jai prakashnarayan. N. T. Ramarao, M. G. Ramchandran, Jaylalita.

The Great Political  Leaders and Martyrs..

Mahatma  Gandhi,  Indira  Gandhi,  Rajiv  Gandhi, Beant Singh

The Great Military Generals..

Field    Marshal    Sammanekshaw,    General JagjitSingh    Arora,    Field    marshal    K.M. cariappa,Lieutenant  General  J.  F.  R.  Jacob,   Marshal Arjan Singh, Lieutenant GeneralPremindrasingh Bhagat, Lieutenant    General    Raj    Mohan    Vohra, GenralBipinchandra  Rawat,  General  Arun  Sridhar Vaidhya.

The Great Brave  MartyrSoldiers Of Indian Army Who Laid Their Lives For The Nation..

Recipients of Param VirChakra..

Major  Somnath  Sharma,  Naik  Jadunath  Singh, Company   Havaldar   Major   Piru   Singh,   Captain Gurubachan  Singh  Salariya,  SubedarJogindar  Singh, Major Shaitan Singh, Company Quarter Master Havildar Abdul  Hamid,  Lieutenant  Colonel   ArdeshirTarapore, Lance Naik Albert Ekka, Flying Officer Nirmaljit Singh Shekkhon,  Second  Lieutenant  Arun  Khetarpal,  Major RamaswamiParmeshwaran,  Lieutenant  Manoj  Kumar

Pandey, Captain Vikram Batra. Lieutenant Ved Prakash Trehan.

Recipients of MahaVir Chakra..

Lieutenant Colonel Dewan Ranjit Rai, Sepoy Dewan singh Danu, Naik Chandsingh Subedar Bishan Singh, Jemadar Nandsingh, Lieutenant Colonel IJS Butalia, Brigadier Mohamad Usman , Brigadier Rajendra Singh , Major Annavi Krishnaswamy Ramaswamy, Major Sardar Malkit Singh Brare, Major Satyapal Chopra, Subedar Gurudial Singh, Naik Sis Pal Singh , Rifleman Dhonkal Singh, Jemadar HardevSingh, Naik Nar Singh, Subedar Chuna Ram, Jemadar Sampooran Singh, Lance Naik Rabilal Thapa, Captain Dara Dinshaw Mistry, lance Naik Ran Bahadur Gurung,NaikMahabir Thapa, Naik Chain Singh, Havildar Saroop Singh, Second Lieutenant Gopalsingh, krishnaVenketesa Prasanna Rao, Lieutenant Sardul Singh  Randhawa, Sepoy Kewal Singh, Havildar StanzinPhunchok, Jemadar IshtTundup, Rifleman Jaswant Singh Rawat, Major shyamal Dev Goswamy, Major General Sushil Kumar Mathur, Major Baljit Singh Randhawa, Squadron Leader Ajjamada B. Devaiah, Captain Anuj Nayyar, Major Rajesh Singh Adhikari, Captain Keishing CliffordNongrun, Captain NeikezhakuoKenguruse, Major Padmpani Acharya, Major Vivek Gupta, Captain Gurjinder Singh Suri, Colonel B. Santosh Babu

The Great  Brave Soldiers of Indian Army Who served with great bravery  for the nation..

Recipients of Param VirChakra..

Second  Lieutenant  Rama  RaghobaRane,  Lance Naik  Karam  Singh,  Major  Dhan  Singh  Thapa,  Major HoshirsinghDahia, Naib Subedar Bana Singh, Grenadier Yogendra sing Yadav, Rifleman Sanjay Kumar.

Recipients of MahaVirChakra..

Civilian  Ram  Chandar,  Major  Yadunathsingh, Lieutenant Colonel Khushal Chand, Lieutenant General Man Mohan Khanna, Lieutenant Colonel Thakur Prithi Chand, Sepoy  Mansingh,  Havildar  Dayaram,  Colonel Kishansingh  Rathore,  Subedar  Major  and  Honorary Captain  Krishna  Sonawale,   Lieutenant  Colonel  hari Chand, Sepoy Hari Singh, Major General Rajinder Singh Sparrow,  Brigediar  Arvind  NilkanthJater,  Lieutenant Colonel  Kaman  Singh,  Jemadar  Lal  Bahadur  Khattri, Naik  Raju,  Civilian  Porter  Mohd  Ismail,  Sepoy  Amar Singh,  Major  ChewangRinchen,  Naik  Pritam  Singh, Brigadier  Sher  Jung  Thapa,  Subedar  and  Honorary Captain  Fateh  Singh,  Lieutent  Colonel  Harbans  sing Virk, Lieutenant General Anil Krishna Barat, Lieutenant Colonel  Dharam  Singh,  major  General  Anant  Singh Pathania,  Havildar  Ram  Prasad  Gurung,  Jemadar  Lal Singh,  Brigadier  Kanhya  Lal  Atal,  Air  Commodore Mehar Singh, Air marshal MinooMerwan Engineer, Wing

Commander SB Noronha, Lieutenant Colonel AG Rangaraj, Colonel Nirod Baran Banerjee, Air Chief Marshal HrushikeshMoolgavakar, Wing Commander Jag Mohan Nath, Subedar Kanshi Ram, Lieutenant Colonel BhagwanDutt Dogra, Lieutenant Colonel Gurudial Singh, Captain MahabirPrasarandhawa, Major mahendra Singh Chaudhary, Brigadier Sher Pratap Singh Shrikent, Subedar Sonam Stobdn, General Tapish, war Narain Raina, Naib Subedar(Honorary Subedar ) Rabi Lal Thapa, Colonel Ajit Singh, Major General Bejoy Mohan Bhattacharjea , Captain ChanderNarain Singh, Major General Sarup Singh Sangha, Lieutenant General Ranjit Singh Dyal , major Bhaskar Roy, Air Commodore William Mac Donald Goodman, Subedar Ajit Singh, Brigadier Desmond Hayde, Major GurubakshSingh,Lieutenant General Har Krishen Sibel, lieutenant General Khem karan Singh, Lieutenant Colonel Narindera Nath Khanna, Wing Commander Padmanabha Gautam , Air Marshal PremPalSingh, Brigadier RaghubirSingh,Lieutenant Colonel Harbans Lal Mehta, Naib Subeda ( Honorary Subedar ) Naubat Ram.

Brigedier Thomas Krishnan Theogaraj, Major Mohindar Singh, BrigedierSampuran Singh, Major General Salim Caleb, Major General Madan Mohan Singh Bakshi, General Arun Shridhar Vaidya,MajorAsharam Tyagi, Captain Kapil Singh Thapa, Brigadier PagadalaKuppuswamyNandagopal, Subedar Tika Bahadur Thapa, Major Bhupinder Singh, Naik Darshan Singh, Captain Gautam Mumbayi, Brigadier Sant Singh,

Major Harbhajan Singh, Brigadier Rai Singh, Lieutenant Colonel Mahatma Singh, Lieutenant General Anand Sarup, Brigedier Arun BhimaraoHarolikar, Major General hardev Singh kaler, Captain Mohan Narayan Rao Samant, Brigadier Rajkumar Singh, Lieutenant Colonel Surinder kapur, Lance Naik Ram Ugrah Pandey, Sepoy Ansuya Prasad, Rifleman PatiramGaurang, Major Shamsher Singh, Vice Admiral Swaraj Parkash , Major Anup Singh Gahlaut,Brigadier Basdev Singh Mankotia, Major General  Ananat Vishwanath Natu, Major General Kahmiri Lal Rattan, Major General Prem Kumar khanna, Leitenant Colonel Jaivir Singh, Air Vice marshal Vidya Bhushan Vashisht, Group Captain Allan Albert D'Costa, Subedar major and Honorary Captain Bir Bahadur Pun, Commodore KasargodPatnashetti Gopal Rao, Commodore Babrubhan Yadav, Captain Devinder Singh Ahlawat, Lieutenant General Krishnaswamy Gowri Shankar, Brigediar  Kuldip Singh Chandpuri, Brigadier narinder Singh Sandhu, Air Marshal Ravinder Nath Bhardwaj, Lieutenant Colonel Sawai Bhawani Singh, Lieutenant General Joginder Singh Gharaya.

Brigadier Kailash Prasad Pandey, Brigadier Mohinder Lal Whig, Sepoy Pandurang Salunkhe, Air Vice Marshal Chandan Singh, Lieutenant Colonel Chittoor Venugopal, Lieutenant Joginder Singh Bakshi, Subedar major Mohinder Singh, Petty Officer Chiman Singh, Joseph Pius Alfred Noronha, BrigediarUdai Singh Bhati,CaptainMahendranath Mulla, Naik Sugan Singh, Brigadier Rattan Nath Sharma ,Lieutenant Colonel Harish Chandra Pathak, Major Kulwant Singh Pannu,

Brigadier Sukhjit Singh, Major Vijay Rattan Choudhry, lance Naik Drig Pal Singh, Captain Pradipkumar Gour, Brigadier Amarjit Singh Bal, Havildar and Honorary Captain Thomas Philipose,Lieutenant Colonel Ved Prakash Ghai, Leutenant Colonel Hanut Singh, Lieutenant General Raj Mohan Vohra,Captain Shankar Rao Shankhapan, Walkar, Air Vice Marshal Cecil Vivian Parker, Air Commodore Harcharan Singh Manget, Air Vice Marshal Madhvendra Banerji, Subedar Malkiat Singh.

Group Captain Manmohan Bir  Singh Talwar, Air Commodore Ramesh SakharamBenegal, Second Lieutenant Samser Singh Samra, Lance Naik Shanghara Singh, Lance Havildar Dil Bahadur Chettri, Rear Admiral Santosh Kumar Gupta, Brigadier Vijay kumar Berry, Air Chief Marshal S. K. kaul, Subedar Nar Bahadur Chhetri, Colonel Dharam Vir Singh, , Major Daljitsingh Narang, Lieutenant General Ved  Prakash Airy, Assistant Commandant Ram Krishna Wadhwa, Lieutenant Colonel PuttichandaSomaiah Ganapathi, Brigadier Manjit Singh, Lieutenant Arvind Singh, Colonel Keishna Gopal Chatterjee, Lance Havildar  Nar Bahadur Ale , Naik Prem Bahadur Gurung ,Subedar Sansar Chand.

Lieutenant Colonel Inder Bal Singh Bawa, Second Lieutenant Rajeev Sandhu, Captain Pratap Singh, Colonel Vijay Kumar Bakshi, Major Balwan Singh, Lieutenant Colonel Sonam Wangchuk, Naik Digendra Kumar, Sepoy ImliakumAo.

The Great  Martyrs from Police force..

K.   C.   Surendra   Babu,   mallikarjunBande, Avindersing  Brar,  Vinod  Chaubey,  Debashish  Shethy, Eric  Charles  Handyside,  Ashok  Kamte,  Hemant karkare, Kamlesh  Kumari,  Vinod  Kumar  Mehta,  Tukaram  Omble, Vijay  Salaskar,  Pramod  Kumar  Satapathy,  Mohan Chand  Sharma,  Ajay  kumar  Singh,  Ajit  Singh,  Randhir Prasad Verma.


The Great Teachers..

Chanakya,  Sarvapalli  Radhakrishnan,  Savitribai phule,        Dr.        A.        P.        J.        Abdul kalam,IshwarchandraVidhyasagar,            Rabindranath Tagore,Anand Kumar, Alakh Pande.


The Great Laureates And Poets..

Panini,      Kalidas,Bhas,      Chand      Bardai, Rabindranath  Tagore,  Premchand,  Maithili  Sharan Gupt,  Mahadevi  Verma  ,  Nirala  ,  C.  Subramania Bharti,Narsinh      Mehta,Mirza      Galib,      Rahim, ZhaverChandMeghani,      Bankim  Chandra  Chatterjee, BhartenduHarishchandra,  Amrita  Pritam,  R.  K. Narayan, Rahul Sankrutyayan. Anand Baxi, Shailendra, Gulzar .


Jnanpith Awardees..

G. SankaraKurup, TarashankarBandopadhyay, Umashankar Joshi, KuppaliVenkatappa"Kuvempu", Sumitranandan Pant, FiraqGorakhpuri, VishwanathaSatyanarayan , Bishnu Dey, Ramdhari Singh Dinkar, D. R. Bendre, Gopinath Mohanty, Vishnu SakharamKhandekar, Akilan, Ashapoorna Devi, K. Shivaram Karanth, SachchidanandaVatsyayan,Birendra Kumar Bhattacharya, S.K. Pottekkatt,Amrita Pritam, Mahadevi Verma, Masti Venkatesha Iyengar, ThakazhiSivasankara Pillai, Pannalal Patel, SachidanandaRoutray, VishnuVamanShirwadkar "Kusumagraj",C. Naryana Reddy, QuarratulainHyder, Vinayaka Krishna Gokak, Subhash Mukhopadhyay, Naresh Mehta, Sitakant Mahapatra, U. R. Anantmurthy,M. T. Vasudevan Nair, Mahsweta Devi,Ali Sardar Jafri, Girish karnard, Nirmal Verma, Gurudial Singh, MamoniRaisom Goswami, Rajendra Shah, Jayakanthan, VindaKarandikar, Rehman Rahi, Kunwar Narayan,RavindraKelekar, Satyavrat Shastri, O.N.P.Kurup, Akhlaq Mohammed Khan "Shahryar ",Amarkant, ShrilalSukla, ChandrashekharaKambara, Pratibha Ray, RavuriBhrdhwaja,Kedarnath Singh, BhalchandraNemade, Raghuveer Chaudhari,ShankhaGhosh, Krishna Sobti, Amitav Ghosh, AkkithamAchyuthanNamboothiri, NilamniPhookan.


The Great Maharajas..

Maharani Ahalyabai Holkar of Indore, Maharaj Sayajirao Gaekwad of Baroda , Maharaja Bhagvatsingji of Gondal, MaharajaKrishnkumarSingji of Bhavnagar.

The Great Social Reformers..

Raja RammohanRai. Mahatma JyotibaPhule, Keshav Chandra Sen, Mahadev Govind Ranade, IhswarchandraVidhyasagar, Pandurang Shastri Athavale, VinaobaBhave, Devendranath Tagore, Dhondo Keshav karve,Narayan Guru, Basavanna.

The Great Artists..

Musicians -Singers..

Tansen,BaijuBawra, Tana Riri, Ravishankar,Bismillakhan, Bhimsen Joshi, Lata mangeshkar, Mohmad Rafi, Kishor Kumar, Mukesh, A. R. Raheman, S. D. Burman, R. D. Burman, HariprasadChaurasiya, Zakir Husaain, Shivkumar Sharma, Amzad Ali khan, M . S. Subbalaxmi, Jagjit Singh, Ilaiyaraaja, Yesudas, Manna Dey, Hemant Kumar, Madan Mohan, Laxmikant Pyarelal, BappiLaheri, Shankar Jaykishan, Asha Bhosle, C. Ramchandra, Pradeep, S. P. Balasubrahmanyam,Vishwa Mohan Bhatt, Pandit Jasraj.M. M. Keervani .Ravindra Jain

Painters..

Raja Ravi Verma, Amrita Sher Gil, TyebMehta, S. H. Raza, Satish Gujral, Nandlal Bose, Rabindranath Tagore, Manjit Bawa, Jatin Das, Kanu Desai, Ravishankar Raval, R. K. Laxman ( cartoonist) .

Movie Artists..

Satyajit Ray, Dada Saheb Phalke, Dilip Kumar, Raj Kapoor, Dev Anand,Manoj Kumar, Ashok Kumar,Ajit, Raj Kumar,Vaijyanti Mala, VaheedaRaheman, Dharmendra, Hema Malini, Amitabh Bachhan,Mrunal Sen, RitvikGhatak, Gulzar, Sanjeev Kumar, Irfan, Amitabh Bachhan, Guru Datt, Madhu Bala, Girish karnard, Amol Palekar, N. T. Ramarao, M. G. Ramchandran, Jaylalita.RajaMauli.

The Great Sportsman..

Cricketer..

Sunil Gavaskar, Sachin Tendulkar, Kapil Dev, Mahendra Singh Dhoni, Mohammad Azharuddin, Saurav Ganguli, Ravindra jadeja, Rahul Dravid, DilipVengsarkar, Ravi Shastri, Harbhazan Singh, GundappaVishwnath, Syed Kirmani.

Other sports ..

P. T . Usha, Vishwanathan Anand, Milkha singh, Saina Nehwal, Pragyananda

Olympic Winners..

Norman Pritchard, K. D. Jhadhav, Leander Paes, karnammalleswari, Rajyavardhan Singh Rathod, Abhinav Bindra, Vijendra Singh, Sushil Kumar, Vijay Kumar, Saina Nehwal, Mary Kom, Gagan Narang, Yogeshwar Dutt, P. V. Sindhu, Sakshi Malik, Neeraj Chopra, SikhomMirabaiChanu, Ravi Kumar Dahiya, , LovlinaBorgohain, Bajrang Punia . And Hockey Team Several Times.

Olympic Hockey Players..

Leslie Claudius, Udham Singh, Richard James Allen, DhyanChand,RangnathanFrnacis, Randhir Singh Gentle, Balbir Singh Sr. , Shankar Lakshman, Haripal Kaushik, John Peter, Prithipal Singh, Harbinder Singh, Carlyle Tapscll,Roop Singh, Jaswant Rai, Govind Perumal, Amir Kumar, Jaswant Singh Rajput, Leslie Hammond, Broome Pinniger, Sayed Jaffar,Keshav Dutt, Grahandndan Singh ,K. D. Singh, Raghbir Lal, Joginder Singh, Charanjit Singh, Raghbir Singh Bhola, Mohinder Lal, Balkrishna Singh, Rajendran Christie, BalbirSinghKullar, Jagjit Singh,Gurubax Singh, Krishnamurthy Perumal,Ajitpal Singh, Harmik Singh.

The Great Industrialists..

Jamshedji Tata, Ghanshyam Das Birla, Jamnalal Bajaj, Dhirubhai Ambani, Azim Premji, WalchandHirachand, Niranjan Hiranandani, Gautam Adani, Pankaj Patel, karsanbhai Patel, Tulsi Tanti, HabilKhorakiwala, Jagdishchandra and kailashchandra Mahindra, Aditya Mittal, B. V. R. Mohan Reddy, B. V. Rao, KailasamRaghvendra Rao, K.I. Varaprasad Reddy, Arvind Mafatlal.

The Great Doctors

Dr. Bidhan Chandra Roy,Dr. DwarkanathKotnis, Dr. AnandiJoshi , Dr. UpendranathBrahmchari.

The Great Engineers..

Sir MokshagundamVisvesvaraya, Bhai kaka, ElattuvalapilSreedharan, VergheseKurien, Kalpana Chawla, Vinod Dham, Satya nadella, Sundar Pichai, A. N. Khosla, Raghuram Govind Rajan, Narayana Murthy, Priya Balasubramaniam,Thomas kailath, ChewangNorphel, ChandrakumarNaranbhai Patel.

The Great Scientists..

Aryabhataa, Bhaskaracharya, C. V. Raman, Srinivas Ramanujan, Prafulla Chandra Ray,Prasatn Chandra Mahalonibus, Dr. Vikram Sarabhai, Satish

Dhawan, M. S. Swaminathan,A. P. J. Abdul kalam, Sam Pitroda , Homi Bhabha.

The Great Civil servants..

K. Subramanya, Ajit Doval, B. N. Rau, T. N. Sheshan, K. P. S . Gill, JulioRebeiro,  Kiran Bedi, S. R. Sankaran, Anna Ranam Malhotra, Vinod Rai.

The Great Social Workers..

Vinoba Bhave, Kailash Satyarthi, Baba Amte, ArunaRoy ,Ansu Gupta, Ela Bhatt.

ThoseWho May Not Have Borne In India -But Becomes Her Beloved Sons Or Daughters And Loved And Respected Indian Culture ..

Lord Louis Mountbatten, Allan Octavian Hume, Lieutenant-Colonel James Tod, David Frawley,Francois Gautier,Mother Teresa , Mother -MirraAlfssa (accompanied Maharshi Arvind ), Miraben -Madeleine Slade ( accompanied mahtma Gandhi ), Sister Nivedita-Margaret Elizabeth Noble (Accompanied Swami Vivekananda),Annie besant, Rennelynn,Maria Wirth, Karolina Goswami, KoenraadElst, GaieaSanskrit,Jonas Masetti, Cassandra Mae Spittmann.

This list is infinite and without end.The horizons of this  list ever expanding day by day as the time passes.

The preparation of  complete, perfect and full list is beyond someone's capacity -as so that is beyond the capacity of author too. Deeply apologizing for the mistake,  error and incompleteness of this list.But it is just  an small effort, to give glimpses- and to introduce at least- the names- of the some of the  great sons-among all of such great sons- of this soil to the readers.

There are so many great sons have borne in India who love and served Motherland India to best of their ability and capacity-we respect,remember, honor, paying homage and paying tribute to them all..

Again Let's bow down and respect,remember, pay our homage and tribute to  those great people  with deep feelings respect and love from  our heart..

# ANCIENT VEDIC PRAYERS

***

ॐ असतो मा सद्गमय ।
तमसो मा ज्योतिर्गमय ।
मृत्योर्मा अमृतं गमय ।
ॐ शान्तिः शान्तिः शान्तिः ॥

Omasato masadgamaya।
Tamasomājyotirgamaya।
Mrutyormaamrutangamaya।
Aum shantiahshantiahshantiah॥

Aum Lead us from the unreal to the real
Lead us from darkness to light
Lead us from death to immortality
Aum peace, peace, peace!

***

ॐ सह नाववतु ।
सह नौ भुनक्तु ।
सह वीर्यं करवावहै ।
तेजस्वि नावधीतमस्तु मा विद्विषावहै ।
ॐ शान्तिः शान्तिः शान्तिः ॥

Aum sahnavavatu।
Sah naubhunaktu।
Sah viryankaravavahai।
Tejasvinavadhitamastu mavidvishavahai।

Aum shantiahshantiahshantiah॥

Om, Together may we Move
Together may we  Relish
Together may we perform  Vigor
May what has been Studied by us be Brilliance
May it Not give rise to Hostility
Om Peace, Peace, Peace.

***

ॐ सर्वे भवन्तु सुखिनः
सर्वे सन्तु निरामयाः।
सर्वे भद्राणि पश्यन्तु मा कश्चिद्दुःखभाग्भवेत।
ॐ शान्तिः शान्तिः शान्तिः॥

Aum sarvebhavantusukhinah
Sarvesantuniramayaah।
Sarvebhadraṇipashyantu
makashchidduahkhabhagbhaveta।
Aum shantiahshantiahshantiah॥

May all sentient beings be at peace,
may no one suffer from illness,
May all see what is auspicious, may no one suffer.
Om peace, peace, peace.

***

*ऋग्वेद - मंडल १० -सूक्त १९१ (संज्ञानसूक्त)*

सं समिध्वसे वृषन्नग्रे विश्वान्यर्य आ ।
ईळस्पदे समिधुवसे स नो वसुन्या भर ॥१॥

48

संगच्छध्वं संवदध्वं
सं वो मनांसि जानताम्
देवा भागं यथा पूर्वे
सञ्जानाना उपासते ॥२॥

समानो मन्त्र: समिति: समानी
समानं मन: सहचित्तमेषाम्
समानं मन्त्रमभिमन्त्रये व:
समानेन वो हविषा जुहोमि ॥३॥

समानी व आकूति: समाना हृदयानि व: |
समानमस्तु वो मनो यथा व: सुसहासति ॥४॥

San samidhavasevṛuṣhannagnevishvanyarya a ।
ilaspadesamidhuvase s no vasunyabhar॥1॥

Sangachchhadhvansanvadadhvan
San vomanaansijanatam
Devabhaganyathapurve
Sanyjananaupasate॥2॥

Samano mantra: samiti: samani
Samanan mana: sahachittameṣham
Samananmantramabhimantrayeva:
Samanenvohaviṣhajuhomi॥3॥

Samani v akuti: samanahṛudayaniva: |
Samanamastuvo mano yathava: susahasati॥4॥

Oh desired fruitful fire, having united everyone from all
directions, sit in the middle of the sacrificial altar and sit
there, draw wealth for us.(1)

May you all together go.
May all of you together speak also.
May your minds further
be the same unanimously,
as the ancient deities unitedly
accept their own sacrificial share. (2)

Let their hymnal praise be the same.
The same let their assembly be.
Let their mind be the same.
Let their thoughts be the same unitedly.
I'm uttering your same incantation.
I'm also performing
the sacrificial offering
with your same oblation.(3)

Let your perseverance of all be the same.
Let all your hearts be the same.
The same let your mind be,
so that a nice company yours would be. (4)

***

सत्यमेव जयते नानृतं सत्येन पन्था विततो देवयानः।
येनाक्रमंत्यृषयो ह्याप्तकामो यत्र तत्सत्यस्य परमं निधानम्॥

मुंडकउपनिषद (३-१-६)

"satyamevjayatenanṛutansatyenpanthavitatodevayana
hι

Yenakramantyruṣhayohyaptakamo yatra
tatsatyasyaparamannidhanamιι

Ultimately, truth triumphs, not falsehood. This is the path by which the sages who have fulfilled their desires attain the ultimate goal of life.

सत्यमेव जयते ॥is Indias National Motto

***

,"उप सर्प मातरं भूमिमेतामुरुव्यचसं पृथिवीं सुशेवां"

"upsarpamaatarambhumimetamuruvyachasanpruthiviansusheva an"

"O man! Serve this vast land of happiness,  continuously with the same respect as your mother. "(Rigveda 10-18-10)

***

"यतेमहि स्वराज्ये"

"yatemahisvarajye"

"Let us always strive for Swarajya ( Rigveda 5-66-6)

***

"सासह्याम पृतन्यतः"

"sasahyamprutanyatah"

"Victory over invaders" (Rigveda 1-8-4)

***

"आ ब्रह्मन् ब्राह्मणो ब्रह्मवर्चसी जायतामा राष्ट्रे राजन्यः
शूरऽइषव्योऽतिव्याधी महारथो जायतां दोग्ध्री धेनुर्वोढाऽनड्वाना शुः
समिः पुरन्धिर्योषा जिष्णू रथेष्ठाः सभेयो युवास्य यजमानस्य वीरो
जायतां निकामे नः पर्जन्यो वर्षतु फलवत्यो नऽओषधयः पच्यन्तां
योगक्षेमो नः कल्पताम्"

"a brahman
brahmaṇoanbrahmavarchasijayatamarashṭrerajanyahshura'iṣhav
yo'tivyadhimaharathojayataandogdhridhenurvoḍhaa'naḍvanashu
ahsaptiahpurandhiryoṣhajiṣhṇaratheṣhṭhaahsabheyoyuvasyayaja
mānasyavirojayataannikame nah
parjanyovarṣhatufalavatyonaoṣhadhayahpachyantaanyogakṣhe
mo nah kalpatam"

Hey Brahman! May our nation be blessed with
knowledgeable in brahamn , brave warriors, warrior-
rulers who suppress the enemy, capable animals like milk-
giving cows and horses. May there be virtuous women,
civilized people, may there be sufficient rain as per
expectation, may there be trees laden with fruits, flowers,
grains and medicines.

(Yajurveda 22-22)

***

"नमो मात्रे पृथिव्यै नमो मात्रे पृथिव्याऽइयं ते राड्यन्तासि यमनो
ध्रुवोऽसि धरुण:। कृष्यै त्वा क्षेमाय त्वा रय्ये त्वा पोषाय त्वा॥"

"namomatrepruthivyainamomatrepruthivyaiyanteradya
ntasiyamanodhruvosidharuṇa: ।
kṛuṣhyaitvakṣhemayatvarayyetvaposhayatvaǁ"

Our salutations to Mother Earth, our salutations again, going beyond the territorial boundaries of the country, let us for mutual humbelness,dedicate ourselves for the achievement of collective welfare in a spirit of friendship for the benefit of all.

(Yajurveda 9-22)

***

"दीर्घ न आयुः प्रतिबुध्यमाना वयं तुभ्यं बलिहृतः स्याम"

"dirgha n ayuahpratibudhyamanavayantubhyanbalihṛutahsyama"

" Let us Sacrifice our longevity  of  life, for the sake motherland",

(Atharvveda 12-1-62)

***

"तासु नो तेह्य्यभि नः पवस्व माता भूमिः पुत्रो अहं पृथिव्याः"

"tasu no tehyayabhi nah pavasvamatabhumiahputroahanpṛuthivyaah"

The land that protects us from all sides is my mother and
I am her son

(Atharvaveda 12-1-12).

***

"त्यजेत् कुलार्थे पुरुषं ग्रामस्यार्थे कुलं त्यजेत् ।
ग्रामं जनपदस्यार्थे आत्मार्थे पृथिवीं त्यजेत् ॥"

"tyajetkularthepurushamgramasyarthekulamtyajet |
gramamjanapadasyartheatmartheprithivImtyajet ||"

Renounce one person for the sake of the family, a family
for the sake of village; village for the sake of country and
even the [kingdom of] earth for one's own sake.

(From  Mahabharat, Pachtantra and Hitopadesh ,
VidurNiti 5-17 )

मित्राणि धन धान्यानि प्रजानां सम्मतानिव ।
जननी जन्म भूमिश्च स्वर्गादपि गरीयसी ॥

Mitrāṇidhandhānyāniprajānāansammatānivı

Jananījanmabhūmishchasvargādapigarīyasīıı

"Friends, blessed ones, grains, etc, are highly respected in
the world (But) the place of mother and motherland-
birthplace is higher than heaven "

(From Some version of ValmikiRamayan, -Rishi Bhardwaj addressing to Lord Rama)

अपि स्वर्णमयी लङ्का न मे लक्ष्मण रोचते ।
जननी जन्मभूमिश्च स्वर्गादपि गरीयसी ॥
Apisvarṇamayīlankā n me lakṣhmaṇrochate।
Jananījanmabhūmishchasvargādapigarīyasī॥

"Lakshaman! Although this Lanka is made of Gold, yet I have no interest in it (Because) my mother and motherland-birthplace are greater than heaven"
(From Some version of Valmiki Ramayan, -Lord Rama addressing to Lakshaman)

॥ यतो धर्मस्ततो जय ॥

(Quote from Mahabharata ..*Yatodharmstatojay* Where there is righteousness and moral duty (dharma), there is victory (Jayah)) ( This is motto of Supreme Court of India)

# PRAYER ADOPTED BY MAHATMA GANDHI DURING FREEDOM STRUGGLE VAISHNAV JAN TO TENE KAHIYE

This Bhajan-kknown as "Vaishnav Jan To Tene Re Kahiye " A religious prayer which was written in 15th century by Gujarati Poet Narsinh Mehta. This Bhajan was adopted by mahatma Gandhi in Freedom Struggle – and was normally sung during prayers by Gandhiji.

### Original Gujarati Script

વૈષ્ણવ જન તો તેને કહિયેજે પીડ પરાઈ જાણે રે

વૈષ્ણવ જન તો તેને કહિયેજે પીડ પરાઈ જાણે રે

પર દુ:ખે ઉપકાર કરે તો યેમન અભિમાન ના આણે રે

વૈષ્ણવ જન તો તેને કહિયેજે પીડ પરાઈ જાણે રે


સકળ લોકમાં સહુને વંદેનિંદા ન કરે કેની રે

વાચ કાછ મન નિશ્છળ રાખેધન ધન જનની તેની રે

વૈષ્ણવ જન તો તેને કહિયેજે પીડ પરાઈ જાણે રે

સમદૃષ્ટિ ને તૃષ્ણા ત્યાગીપરસ્ત્રી જેને માત રે
જિહ્વા થકી અસત્ય ન બોલેપરધન નવ ઝાલે હાથ રે
વૈષ્ણવ જન તો તેને કહિયેજે પીડ પરાઈ જાણે રે


મોહ માયા વ્યાપે નહિ જેનેદૃઢ વૈરાગ્ય જેના મનમાં રે
રામ નામ શુ તાળી રે લાગીસકળ તીરથ તેના તનમાં રે
વૈષ્ણવ જન તો તેને કહિયેજે પીડ પરાઈ જાણે રે


વણ લોભી ને કપટ રહિત છેકામ ક્રોધ નિવાર્યાં રે
ભણે નરસૈયો તેનું દર્શન કરતાકુળ એકોતેર તાર્યાં રે
વૈષ્ણવ જન તો તેને કહિયેજે પીડ પરાઈ જાણે રે
પર દુ:ખે ઉપકાર કરે તો યેમન અભિમાન ના આણે રે
વૈષ્ણવ જન તો તેને કહિયેજે પીડ પરાઈ જાણે રે

**Hindi  Transliteration**


वैष्णव जन तो तेने कहिये जे पीड़ परायी जाणे रे
वैष्णव जन तो तेने कहिये जे पीड़ परायी जाणे रे
पर दुख्खे उपकार करे तोये मन अभिमान ना आणे रे
वैष्णव जन तो तेने कहिये जे पीड़ परायी जाणे रे

सकळ लोक मान सहुने वंदे निंदा न करे केनी रे
वाच काछ मन निश्चल राखे धन धन जननी तेनी रे
वैष्णव जन तो तेने कहिये जे पीड़ परायी जाणे रे

सम दृष्टी ने तृष्णा त्यागी पर स्त्री जेने मात रे
जिह्वा थकी असत्य ना बोले पर धन नव झाली हाथ रे
वैष्णव जन तो तेने कहिये जे पीड़ परायी जाणे रे

मोह माया व्यापे नही जेने द्रिढ़ वैराग्य जेना मन मान रे
राम नाम शु ताळी लागी सकल तिरथ तेना तन मान रे
वैष्णव जन तो तेने कहिये जे पीड़ परायी जाणे रे

वण लोभी ने कपट- रहित छे काम क्रोध निवार्या रे
भणे नरसैय्यो तेनुन दर्शन कर्ता कुळ एकोतेर तारया रे
वैष्णव जन तो तेने कहिये जे पीड़ परायी जाणे रे
पर दुख्खे उपकार करे तोये मन अभिमान ना आणे रे
वैष्णव जन तो तेने कहिये जे पीड़ परायी जाणे रे

## English Transliteration

Vaiṣhṇavjan to tenekahiye je pidpaayijaṇe re
Vaiṣhṇavjan to tenekahiye je pidparāyijaṇe re
Par dukhkheupakarkaretoye man abhimānnaane re
Vaiṣhṇavjan to tenekahiye je pīdparayajaṇe re
Sakaḷlok man sahunevandenianda n karekeni re
Vachkachh man nishchalrakhedhandhanjananiteni re
Vaishnav jan to tenekahiye je pidparayi jane re
Sam drushṭi ne tṛuṣhṇatyagi par strijene mat re
Jihvathakiasatyana bole par dhan nav zali hath re
Vaiṣhṇavjan to tenekahiye je pidparayi jane re
Moh mayavyapenahijenedridha vairagya jena man man re
Rāmnām sun talilagisakaltirathtena tan man re
Vaiṣhṇavjan to tenekahiye je pidparayi jane re
Vaṇlobhi ne kapaṭa- rahitchhekamkrodhnivarya re
Bhaṇenarasaiyyotenun darshan kartakuḷekotertaraya re
Vaiṣhṇavjan to tenekahiye je pidparayijaṇe re
Par dukhkheupakarkaretoye man abhimannaane re
Vaiṣhṇavjan to tenekahiye je pidparayi jane re

## English Translation

Call those people Vaishnavas,
who feel the pain of others.
Help those who are sad,
but never let ego enter your mind.
Those who respect the whole world,
do not condemn anyone.
Keep your words, actions and thoughts pure,
his mother is blessed.
One who sees everyone with equal vision, abandons craving,
knows other women as mother.
Whose tongue never utters false words,
whose hands never touch other's wealth.
Those who do not bow down before worldly temptations,
who have firm disinterest in their mind.
Those who are fascinated by the name of Ram,
all the places of pilgrimage are included in them only.
Those who have given up greed and deceit,
who stay away from lust and anger.
Narsi says: I will be grateful to meet such a soul,
by whose virtue his whole family becomes free.॥

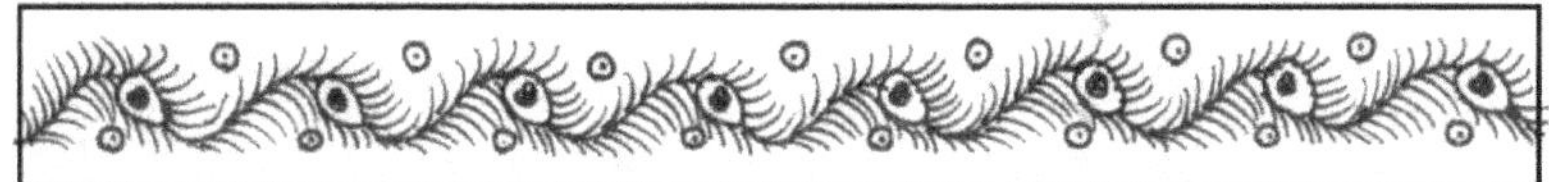

# ALL RELIGION PRAYER

This All-Religion Prayer was composed by Vinoba Bhave.

## Hindi Script

ॐ तत्सत् श्री नारायण तुं,पुरुषोत्तम गुरु तुं;

सिद्ध बुद्ध तुं, स्कन्द विनायकसविता पावक तुं,

ब्रह्म मजद तुं, यह्व शक्ति तुं,इसु पिता प्रभु तुं

रुद्र विष्णु तुं, राम-कृष्ण तुं,रहीम ताओ तुं,

वासुदेव गो-विश्वरूप तुं,चिदानन्द हरि तुं;

अद्वितीय तुं, अकाल निर्भयआत्म-लिंग शिव तुं

ॐ तत्सत् श्री नारायण तुं,पुरुषोत्तम गुरु तुं;

## English Transliteration

Om tat sat srinarayanatu
Purushothama guru tu
Siddha buddha tu, skandavinayaka
Savita pavakatu, savitapavakatu

brahma mazdatu, yahvashakthitu
Yeshupitha prabhu tu

Rudra vishnutu, ramakrishnatu
Rahim taotu, rahimtaotu

vasudeva go vishwaroopatu
Chidanandaharitu
Advitiyatu akala nirbhaya
Atmalinga shiva tu
Om tat sat srinarayanatu
Purushothama guru tu

**English Translation**

Om, you are that, you are Narayana, God in human
form;
You are the embodiment of perfection and the perfect
teacher.
You are the enlightened Buddha; You are Skand-
Subrahmanya and Ganesha, the remover of obstacles;
You are the sun-fire that destroys the darkness of
ignorance.

You are Brahma, the creator; Mazda, great one. You are
Jehovah, and the Divine Mother, the creative energy.
You are Jesus, our Lord, Holy Father.
You are Rudra, the changer and Vishnu, the preserver;
You are Rama and Krishna;
You are Rahim, the All Merciful, the Ever Giving and the
Expansive; you are tao.

You are Vasudev, the maintainer of all, omnipotent and
omnipresent;

You are Hari, the destroyer of illusions, the blissful soul.
You are unique and one of a kind, beyond time and
fearless of adversity;
You are Shiva, the Atma Lingam, the symbol of the
formless Absolute.
Om, you are that, you are Narayana, God in human
form;
You are the embodiment of perfection and the perfect
teacher.

# CHAPTER -1
# SCRIPTS OF NATIONAL IMPORTANCE

## 1.1 PREAMBLE TO THE CONSTITUTION OF INDIA

**WE, THE PEOPLE OF INDIA** having solemnly resolved to constitute India into a **SOVEREIGN SOCIALIST SECULAR DEMOCRATIC REPUBLIC** and to secure to all its citizens:

**JUSTICE,** social, economic and political;

**LIBERTY** of thought, expression, belief, faith and worship;

**EQUALITY** of status and of opportunity; and to promote among them all

**FRATERNITY** assuring the dignity of the individual and the unity and integrity of the Nation;

IN OUR CONSTITUENT ASSEMBLY this twenty-sixth day of November, 1949, do **HEREBY ADOPT, ENACT AND GIVE TO OURSELVES THIS CONSTITUTION.**

## 1.2  NATIONAL MOTTO

सत्यमेव जयते।

"satyamevjayate"

## TRUTH ALONE TRIUMPHS

## 1.3 (OATH OF ALLEGIANCE )

## INDIA'S NATIONAL PLEDGE

India is my country and all Indians are my brothers and sisters.
I love my country and I am proud of its rich and varied heritage.
I shall always strive to be worthy of it.
I shall give respect to my parents, teachers and all elders and treat everyone with courtesy.
To my country and my people, I pledge my devotion. In their well-being and prosperity alone lies my happiness.

## 1.4 NATIONAL ANTHEM

( The National Anthem- Composed by Rabindranath Tagore(1861-1941)- Bengali Poet and laureate   )

जन-गण-मन-अधिनायक जय हे, भारतभाग्यविधाता!
पंजाब- सिन्ध -गुजरात -मराठा ,द्राविड़- उत्कल- बंग
विन्ध्य हिमाचल यमुना गंगा, उच्छलजलधितरंग
तव शुभ नामे जागे, तव शुभ आशिष मागे
गाहे तव जयगाथा।
जन-गण-मंगलदायक जय हे, भारतभाग्यविधाता!
जय हे!जय हे !जय हे ! जय जय जय जय हे।।

**Jana Gana Mana Lyrics**

Jana –Gana- Mana Adhinaayak Jaya Hey,
BhaaratBhaagyaVidhaataa!
Panjaab–Sindha- Gujarat -Maraatha,
Draavid Utkal Banga
Vindhya Himaachal Yamuna Ganga,
UchchhalJaladhi Taranga
TavShubhNaameyJaagey,
TavShubh Aashish Maange
GaaheyTavJayagaathaa.
Jana -Gana-Mangal Daayak,
Jaya Hey BhaaratBhaagyaVidhaataa!
Jaya Hey!Jaya Hey! Jaya Hey!
Jaya JayaJaya, Jaya Hey!

**Jana Gana Mana - English Translation**

"Thou art the ruler of the minds of all people,
Dispenser of India's destiny.
Thy name rouses the hearts of Punjab, Sindh,
Gujarat and Maratha,
Of the Dravida, Orissa and Bengal;

It echoes in the hills of the Vindhyas and Himalayas,
mingles in the music of Jamuna and Ganges and is
chanted by the waves of the Indian Sea.
They pray for thy blessings and sing thy praise.
The saving of all people waits in thy hand,
Thou dispenser of India's destiny.
Victory, victory, victory to thee."

(A formal rendition of the national anthem takes
approximately 52 seconds.  - Observance of proper
decorum  as per Government of Indis Guidelines to be
followed. When It is sung all should stand up in respect)

## 1.5 NATIONAL SONG

( National song was written by Bankim Chandra
Chatterjee-(1838-1894) Bengali poet and laureate,  The
first two verses of the poem were adopted as the National
Song of India )

वन्दे मातरम, वन्दे मातरम।
सुजलाम् सुफलाम् मलयजशीतलाम्,
शस्यश्यामलाम मातरम। वन्दे मातरम्॥
शुभ्रज्योत्स्नाम पुलकितयामिनीम्,
फुल्लकुसुमित द्रुमदलशोभिनीम्,
सुहासिनीम् सुमधुरभाषिणीम्,
सुखदाम् वरदाम् मातरम्।

वन्दे मातरम्,वन्दे मातरम्॥

**English Transliteration**

VandemataramIVandemataramI

Sujalamsufalammalayajashitalam,

ShasyashyamalammataramI vandemataramII


Shubhrajyotsnapulakitayaminam,

Fullakusumitdrumadalashobhinim,

Suhasinimsumadhurabhaṣhiṇim,

SukhadamvaradammataramI

VandemataramIvandemataramII

**English Translation**

Mother, I bow to thee!
Rich with thy hurrying streams,
Bright with thy orchard gleams,
Cool with the winds of delight,
Dark fields waving, Mother of might,
Mother free.


Glory of moonlight dreams,
Over thy branches and lordly streams,
Clad in thy blossoming trees,
Mother, giver of ease,
Laughing low and sweet,
Mother, I kiss thy feet,
Speaker sweet and low,
Mother, to thee I bow.

## 1.6 NATIONAL SONG VANDE MATRARAM
## FULL SCRIPT

वन्दे मातरम.वन्दे मातरम।
सुजलाम् सुफलाम् मलयजशीतलाम्,
शस्यश्यामलाम् मातरम्। वन्दे मातरम्।।

शभ्रज्योत्स्नाम पलकितयामिनीम्,
फुल्लकुसमित द्रमदलशोभिनीम्,
सुहासिनीम् सुमधुरभाषिणीम्,
सुखदाम् वरदाम् मातरम्। वन्दे मातरम्।।

सप्त-कोटि- कण्ठ कल-कल निनाद कराले,
द्विसप्त-कोटि- भजैर्धृत खरकरवाले,
अबला केन मा एत बॉले,
बहुबलधारिणीं नमामि तारिणीम्,
रिपुदलवारिणीं मातरम्। वन्दे मातरम्।।

तुमि विद्या तुमि धर्म,
तुमि हृदि तुमि मर्म,
त्वम हि प्राणाः
शरीरे.बाहते तुमि माँ शक्ति,
हृदये तुमि माँ भक्ति,
तोमारेई प्रतिमा गड़ि मन्दिरे-मन्दिरे। वन्दे मातरम्।।

त्वम् हि दुर्गा दशप्रहरणधारिणी,
कमला कमलदलविहारिणी,
वाणी विद्यादायिनी, नमामि त्वाम्,
नमामि कमलाम् अमलाम् अतुलाम्,
सुजलां सुफलां मातरम्। वन्दे मातरम्।।

श्यामलाम् सरलाम् सुस्मिताम् भूषिताम्,
धरणीम् भरणीम् मातरम्।

वन्दे मातरम्, वन्दे मातरम्।।

**English Transliteration**
Vandemataram।Vandemataram।
Sujalamsufalammalayajashitalam,
Shasyashyamalammataram। vandemataram।।

Shubhrajyotsnapulakitayaminim,
Fullakusumitdrumadalashobhinim,
Suhasinimsumadhurabhashinim,
Sukhadamvaradammataram। vandemataram।।

Sapt-kantha kala-kalninadkarale,
Dwisapt-kotibhujairdhrutkharakaravale,
Abala kena ma eta bale!
Bahubaladhariniannamamitarinim,
Ripudalavarinianmataram। vandemataram।।

Tumi vidyatumi dharma,
Tumi hruditumimarma,
Tvam hi praṇaahsharire,

Bahutetumi manshakti,
Hrudayaetumi manbhakti,
Tomareipratimagadimandire-
mandireivandematarami l

Tvam hi durgadashapraharanadharini,
Kamalakamaladalaviharini,
Vanividyadayini, namamitvam,
Namamikamalamamalamatulam,
Sujalaansufalaanmatarami vandemataramll

Shyamalamsaralamsusmitambhashitam,
Dharanimbharanimmatarami
VandemataramiVandemataramll

**English Translatation**

Mother, I bow to thee!
Rich with thy hurrying streams,
Bright with thy orchard gleams,
Cool with the winds of delight,
Dark fields waving, Mother of might,
Mother free.

Glory of moonlight dreams,
Over thy branches and lordly streams,
Clad in thy blossoming trees,
Mother, giver of ease,
Laughing low and sweet,
Mother, I kiss thy feet,

Speaker sweet and low,
Mother, to thee I bow. [Verse 1]

Who hath said thou art weak in thy lands,
When the swords flash out in seventy million hands,
And seventy million voices roar
Thy dreadful name from shore to shore?
With many strengths who art mighty and strong,
To thee I call, Mother and Lord!
Thou who savest, arise and save!
To her I cry who ever her foemen drove
Back from plain and Sea
And shook herself free. [Verse 2]

Thou art wisdom, thou art law,
Thou art heart, our soul, our breath
Thou art love divine, the awe
In our hearts that conquers death.
Thine the strength that nerves the arm,
Thine the beauty, thine the charm.
Every image divine.
In our temples is but thine. [Verse 3]

Thou art Goddess Durga, Lady and Queen,
With her hands that strike and her swords of sheen,
Thou art Goddess Kamala (Lakshmi), lotus-throned,
And Goddess Vani (Saraswati), bestower of wisdom
known
Pure and perfect without peer,
Mother lend thine ear,
Rich with thy hurrying streams,
Bright with thy orchard gleams,
Dark of hue O candid-fair [Verse 4]

In thy soul, with jewelled hair
And thy glorious smile divine,
Loveliest of all earthly lands,
Showering wealth from well-stored hands!
Mother, mother mine!
Mother sweet, I bow to thee,
Mother great and free! [Verse 5]

## 1.7 NATIONAL SYMBOLS
### 1.7 (1) Official Name-  Republic Of India –

### भारत गणराज्य (BHARATGANARAJYA )

### 1.7 (2) National Flag- INDIAN TRICOLOUR

A horizontal rectangular tricolour with equally sized deep saffron at the top, white in the middle and India green at the bottom. Saffron colour is a symbol of sacrifice and courage. White colour of National flag represents peace, honesty, and purity. Green colour of National flag represents faith and chivalry, and is a symbol of prosperity, vibrancy, and life. Shape of National Flag shall be in the ratio of 3:2 ( ratio of length to height ). In the center is a navy blue wheel with twenty-four spokes, known as the Ashoka Chakra.

(Protocol -  Display and usage of the flag is governed by the Flag Code of India, 2002 (successor to the Flag Code – India, the original flag code); the Emblems and Names

(Prevention of Improper Use) Act, 1950; and the
Prevention of Insults to National Honor Act,
1971. Insults to the national flag, including gross affronts
or indignities to it, as well as using it in a manner so as to
violate the provisions of the Flag Code, are punishable by
law with imprisonment up to three years, or a fine, or
both.

National Flag Code link :: ( Do Refer with the latest
version )

https://www.mha.gov.in/sites/default/files/flagcodeofindia
_070214.pdf

When Hoisted saffron colour must be always on the top .
and Green at the bottom .

Colour – Top -deep saffron ( Kesari)
Middle – White
Bottom- Indian Green

## 1.7 (3) National Emblem and National Motto

State Emblem of India – Lion Capital of Ashoka.

The State Emblem is an adaptation of the Lion Capital of Asoka at Sarnath. In the original, there are four lions; mounted back to back, on a circular abacus, which itself rests on a bell-shaped lotus. The frieze of the abacus has sculptures in high relief of an elephant, a galloping horse, a bull and a lion separated by intervening **Dharma Chakras.**

The motto Satyameva Jayate, which means 'Truth Alone Triumphs', written in Devanagari script below the profile of the Lion Capital is part of the State Emblem of India

National Motto -**"Satyameva Jayate"** Sanskrit:

"सत्यमेव जयते " ( "Truth Alone Triumphs")

( Attribute of Image –<u>www.wikipaedia.org</u>)

## 1.7 (4) National Anthem – janaGana Mana

## 1.7 (5) National Song – Vandemataram

## 1.7 (6) National Days – Observed every year on the dates mentioned below

## (1) Independecne Day- 15 th August(1947 )

## (2) Republic Day -26$^{th}$January  (1950 )

## (3) Gandhi jayanti- 2$^{nd}$ October (1869)

## 1.7 (7) Shaheed  Diwas –

Matyr'sDay  is observed on 30 th January ( 1948)- Martyrdom  day of Mahatma Gandhi. A two-minute silence in memory of Indian martyrs is observed throughout the country at 11 am. Participants hold all-religion prayers and sing tributes

Martyr's Day is also observed on

23 March (1931)

The anniversary of the deaths of Bhagat Singh, Sukhdev <u>Thapar</u> and Shivaram Rajguru on 23 March 1931, in Lahore, is recognised as a Martyrs' Day

The trio – Bhagat Singh, Shivaram Rajguru, Sukhdev Thapar lost their lives on March 23 in 1931 during the struggle for India's independence and that day in history is celebrated as Martyrs' Day. The trio of heroes was hanged to death.

## 1.7 (8) Indian national Calender – ShalivahanShakaCalender

## 1.7 (9) National Currancy- Indian Rupee

(Attribute of Image – www.wikipaedia.org)

## 1.7 (10) National Flower- Lotus

## 1.7 (11) National Tree- Indian Banyan

## 1.7 (12) National Bird- Indian Peacock

## 1.7 (13) National Fruit- Mango

## 1.7 (14) National Animal- Royal Bengal Tiger

## 1.7 (15) National Heritage Animal- Indian Elephent

# 1.7 (16) National Aquatic Animal – Ganges River Dolphine

# 1.7 (17) National Reptile- King Cobra

# 1.7 (18) National River- Ganga

# 1.7 (19) National Cockade –

IndianNational CockadeA **cockade** is a knot of ribbons, or other circular- or oval-shaped symbol of distinctive colours which is usually worn on a hat ( like a badge) . For India , which is circular in shape and in central there is Green colour in middle ring it is white colour and outer ring it is saffron colour.

Indian National Cockade

(1) Attributes of the Image :The Image reproduced here for information ,awareness and  in respect to Indian National Cockade  :: Originaly created by –Tibetan Pop Rocks,  –

# 1.8 INCRIPTIONS WRITTEN ON AMAR CHAKRA

## AT NATIONAL WAR MEMORIAL

## (FORMERLYAMAR JAWAN JYOTI WAS AT INDIA GATE)

At India Gate Amar jawan Jyoti was Inaugurated on 26th January 1972-By Shrimati Indira Gandhi  , after Indo-Pak War of 1971, Amar Jawan Jyoti . It is with base, Blcak marble pedestal, a cenotaph on top a reversed rifle capped by a war helmet . On all four side of cenotapah "AMAR JAWAN" was written in Gold in Hindi .

# अमर जवान

This Amar Jawan Jyoti was merged with new flame At National War Memorial Inaugrated on 25th February 2019 By Shri Narendra Modi .

This Amar jawan Jyoti was merged with Jyoti of Amar chakra

At National War memorial

Where

# अमर जवान

(Immortal Soldier )

Is written on all four sides

Of Amar chakra and at bottom in front also written in Hindi

शहीदों की चिताओं पर जुड़ेंगे हर बरस मेलें

वतन पर मिटने वालों का यही बाकी निशां होगा ।।

(Gatherings to pay respect, remembrance, homage and tribute will be organized every year on the funeral pyres of the martyrs. This will be the remaining mark of those who die for the country.)

# 1.9 INCRIPTIONS WRITTEN ON INDIA GATE

India Gate was constructed by Brithish, in the memory of Indian soldiers of Indian Army laid their lives in first world war. It was inaugurated in 1931 By Lord Irwin.

The cornice of the India Gate is inscribed with Imperial suns while both sides of the arch have INDIA, flanked by the dates MCMXIV ('1914'; on the left) and MCMXIX ('1919'; on the right). Below the word INDIA, in capital letters, is inscribed:

"TO THE DEAD OF THE INDIAN ARMIES WHO FELL HONOURED IN FRANCE AND FLANDERS MESOPOTAMIA AND PERSIA EAST AFRICA GALLIPOLI AND ELSEWHERE IN THE NEAR AND THE FAR-EAST AND IN SACRED MEMORY ALSO OF THOSE WHOSE NAMES ARE RECORDED AND WHO FELL IN INDIA OR THE NORTH-WEST FRONTIER AND DURING THE THIRD AFGHAN WAR".

On india Gate names of martyr's soldiers inscribed total names are 13313 out of which 12357 were Indians

To remember all brave soldiers - remembering-few representing them whose namesare inscribed on stones of the walls of India Gate ....

Naik Harnam Singh, Lce Naik NimabrSukal, Sepoy Fazal Din , Sepoy Fazal Khan , Sepoy Gayadin Dubey , Sepoy Gopal Singh , Sepoy Haridayal Choubey , Sepoy Hari ram, Sepoy Indrapal Pandey, Sepoy jagnnath Dubey , Sepoy Jagatpal Singh, Sepoy jagdamba Singh , Sepoy Khai Shah, Sepoy Muhhamadkasm, Sepoy Mukhdev Singh , Sepoy Nandkishore Pandey, Sepoy kasim Ali , Sepoy Raju Ram, LceNaik Balwant Singh , Lce Naik kalu Singh, Lce Nail mangtu Singh, Lce Naik naubat Singh, SepuBacchu Singh, Sepoy Bhagat Singh, Sepoy Bhagman Singh, Sepoy Bhagwansingh , Sepoy bhurasingh , Sepoy Biru Singh, Sepoy Chhedu Singh , Sepoy Chhotesingh, Sepoy Dafdar Singh, Sepoy Darshan Singh, Captain M. Clumpha C. D., Lieutenant Keene H. C., SubdrMjrMalkhan Singh, Jemadar Mohar Singh , Drummer Fatta Singh , Follower Jumma, Follower lalta, Follower Net Ram, Sepoy Fazil Rasul khan ,Lce Naik Kunap Deo, Sepoy Mannulal, Gobind sahai, Govind Sawant , Har Chand , Het Ram , Hasim Ali, Jai Ram, Jasu Ram , Sepoy mani Ram, Sepoy Ganga Ram Nanda , Sepoy Ranjit Singh, Sepoy Rawat Singh ,

Sepoy Sanwal Singh, Sepoy Sardar singh, Sepoy SheruSingh, Sepoy Shankar Singh, Sepoy ShiunathSingh, Sepoy Sujan Singh, Sepoy Sukhi Ram Singh, Sepoy Surja Singh, Sepoy Tej Singh Sepoy Tilok Singh, Sepoy Umarao Singh, Sepoy Zahir Singh,

# 1.10 INSCRIPTION MARKED ON JAIPUR COLUMN IN FRONT OF RASHTRAPATI BHAVAN

(At the bottom side of Jaipur Column, On the eastern side is the map of Delhi as then envisioned, while the inscription that runs through three sides of the Column reads. This was drafeted by Lord Irwin - Viceroy of India – This was a modification of the wording originally prposed by Lutyens: Endow your thought with faith, your deeds with courage, your life with service, so all men may know the greatness of India)

**"In thought faith, In word wisdom,<br>In deed courage, In life service<br>So may India be great."**

# 1.11 INSCRIPTIONS WRITTEN ON WALLS AND DOMES OF (PREVIOUS CIRCULAR)PARLIAMENT-SAMVIDHAN SADAN

## INSCRIPTION ON GATE 1

लोरुक द्वारमपात्राण्णू ।
पश्येम त्वां वयं वेरा ॥ (छान्दो 2 -2- 48)

Lorukdvaramapatrarnul
Pashyemtvaanvayan veraⅡ (chhando 2- 2- 48)

" Open the door to thy people

And let us see thee
For the obtaining of  the
Sovereignty." (chhando -2- 2- 48)

## DOME OVER PASSAGE TO CENTRAL HALL. ARABIC QUOTATION

इनलाही ला युगयुयरो माँ बिकीमिन ।
हत्ता युगयुयरो वा बिन नफसे हुम ॥

Inalahi layugayuyaro manbikimin।
Hattayugayuyarova bin nafase hum ॥

"Almighty God will not change the condition of any people unless they bring about a change themselves."

## INSIDE LOKSABHA CHAMBER OVER SPEAKERS CHAIR

धर्मचक्रप्रवर्तनाय ।
Dharmachakrapravartanaya।

"For the rotation of the wheel of righteousness."

## ABOVE THE GATE  OF CENTRAL HALL ,STANZA IN SANSKRIT

अयं निज: परोवेति गणना लघु चेतसाम ।
उदारचारितानां तू वसुधैव कुटुम्बकम् ॥ (पंचतंत्र – ५/३८)

Ayan nija: parovetigaṇanalaghuchetasam।

Udaracharitanaantuvasudhaivkuṭumbakam ॥
(panchatantra – 5/38)

" That one is mine and and the other a stanger is the
concept of little minds. But to the largehearted the
world itself is their family."( Panchtantra-5/38)

## ON THE DOME NEAR LIFT NO1 STANZA FROM MAHABHARATA

न सा सभा यत्र न सन्ति वृद्धाः वृद्धा न ते यो न वदन्ति धर्म म्।
धर्म: स नो यत्र न सत्यमस्ति ,सत्यं न तध्यच्छलमभ्युपैति ॥
महाभारत (५/३५/५८)

N sasabha yatra n santivruddhaahvruddha n teyo n
vadantidharmam।
Dharma: s no yatra n satyamasti satyan n
tadhvachchhalamabhyupaiti॥
Mahabharat (5/35/58)

" That is not an  assembly where there are no elder man
,
Those are not elders, who do not speak with righteousness
That is not righteousness where there is no truth
That is not the truth which one leads one to deceit
Mahabharat."( 5/35/58)

## INSCRIPTION ON DOME NEAR LIFT 2

सभा वा न प्रवेष्टया ,
व्यक्तव्यं वा समजंसम ।
अब्रवन विब्रवन वापी ,
नरो भवति किल्विषी । (मनु ८/१३)

Sabhaya n praveshtaya
Vyaktavyanvasamaiansami
Abruvanvibruvanvani
Narobhavatikilvishii (manu 8/13)

" One must not enter  either an assembly hall,
Or he must speak there with all righteousness,
For one who does not speak or one who speaks falsely,
Does himself in the equal sin involved."

**DOME NEAR LIFT NO. 3 SANSKRIT STANZA**

न हीद्दभं संवननं,
त्रिष लोकेष विध्यते ।
दया मैत्री च भतेष ,
दानं च मधुरा च वाक् ॥

N hiddabhansanvananan,
Trishulokeshuvidhvatei
Dayamaitrichbhuteshu
Dananchmadhurachvakii

" Kindness , friendliness to all ,
Charity and sweet tongue .
Such coincidence has not been found,
( in one oubject ) in all the three worlds. "

**DOME NEAR LIFT NO. 4 SANSKRIT STANZA**

सर्वदा, स्यान्नप: प्राज्ञ :
स्वमते न कदाचन् ।

सम्याधिकारिप्रकृति:
सभास त्सु मते स्थित : ॥

Sarvada  svannapa·pragna :
Svamate n kadachanı
Samvadhikariprakruti·
Sabhastsu mate sthit :॥

" That ruler must ever  have true intelligence,
And he must never be a self- willed man.
All subjects to councilors must he entrust,
Must sit in Assembly and abide by good counse.l "

## DOME NEAR LIFT NO 5 PERSIAN QUOTATION

बरी रुवाक जबंजदं नविश्ता अन्द बजर ,
कि जुज़ निकोई –ए- अहले करम नर वाहद मान्द ।

Bariruvakiabaniadannavishtaandabajar
Ki jujnikoi –e- ahalekaramnarvahadmandaı

" This lofty emerald like building bears the inscription in
gold
Nothing shall last, except the good deeds of the bountiful
"

## DOME NEAR LIFT NO 6SANSKRIT  QUOTATION

प्रजासुखे सुखं राज्ञ: प्रजानां चा हिते हितम् ।
नात्मप्रियं हितं राज्ञ: प्रजानांतु प्रियं हितम् ॥

Prajasukhesukhanragna: prajanaan chahitehitamı

Natmapriyanhitanragna: prajanaantupriyanhitam॥
" In the happiness of his people lies the happiness of
leader , their welfare is his welfare .He shall not consider
as good only that which pleases him but treat as
beneficial to him but treat as beneficial to him  Whatever
causes happiness to all people."

## THE INDIAN PARLIAMENT HAS TWO HOUSES - LOK SABHA AND RAJYA SABHA. THE INSCRIPTION ON THE MAIN ENTRANCE  READS

"Liberty will not descend to a people, a people must raise
themselves to Liberty, it is a blessing that must be earned
before it can be enjoyed".

( Quotation by **Charles Caleb Colton** ( 1777 – 1832))

## 1.12INSCRIPTION ON SENGOL (SCEPTRE -RAJ DANDAM) INSTALLED NEAR SPEAKERS CHAIR IN NEW(TRIANGULAR) PARLIAMENT

Here is a  writup, normally written on sengol during chola
empire in tamilnadu ..

அடியார்கள் வானில் அரசாள்வர் ஆணை நமதே.
Atiyarkalvanilaracalvaranainamate.

It means "It is our order that the follower of the Lord
(Shiva), the king, shall rule as in the heavens"

( Reference-Image Curtsy -Acknowledgements and
Attribute :: The Image shared by Amit Shah-Union
Home Minister of India in  press conference on 24 May
2023 . Conferecne report available on CNN news website
link -
https://twitter.com/CNNnews18/status/166125493430462
8737. The Image reproduced here for information
,awareness and  in respect of Sengol Installed in new
Parliament.
The sengol was crafted in 1947 By jeweller Vummidi
Bangaru Chetty – Chennai )

# 1.13 KING ASHOKAS EDICTS INSCRIPTED IN STONES

( **Ashoka the Great**, was the third emperor of the Maurya Empire of the Indian subcontinent during c. 268 to 232 BCE. His empire covered a large part of the Indian subcontinent. He inscribed many of his edicts on stone across the India. Following is excerpt of his stone edicts )

## 1. KALINGA WAR

"Devanam Priya – Beloved of the Gods, King Piyadasi conquered the Kalingas eight years after his coronation. One lakh fifty thousand were deported, one lakh were killed and many more died (for other reasons). After conquering the Kalingas, the beloved-of -gods felt a strong inclination towards the Dhamma, a love for the Dhamma and a strong inclination for instruction in the Dhamma. Now the Beloved of the Gods deeply repents for having conquered the Kalingas... Now it is victory by Dhamma that the Beloved of the Gods is considered to be the best victory... I have written this Dhamma inscription so that my son and great- Grandsons may not consider making new conquests, or if military conquests are made, they are done with toleration and mild punishment, or even better, that they consider making conquests only by Dhamma, Because it bears fruit in this world and the next. His full devotion should be towards it which will result in this world and the next."

## 2. NONVIOLENCE

"How heavenly signs were absent in the past when the king resorted to violent means to achieve his objectives, but now, after adopting a policy of nonviolence, heavenly signs are again appearing in the form of celestial approval."

## 3. RESPECT FOR ALL RELIGIONS

"Devanama Priya—Beloved of the Gods, King Piyadasi, wants all the Dharma to reside everywhere, as He wants all self-restraint and purity of heart. But people have different desires and different passions, and they can practice all that they should or only part of it. But one who receives great gifts yet lacks self-restraint, purity of heart, gratitude and steadfast devotion, such a person is despicable."

## 4. ALL RELIGIONS ARE EQUAL

"Ashoka condemns the practice of elevating one's own dharma at the expense of someone else's: "Essentially development can be done in various ways, but they all have as their core restraint in speech, i.e. self-righteousness." Do not praise, or condemn the religion of others without good reason. And if there is a reason for criticism, it should be done in a mild manner. But it is better to respect other religions for this reason. is beneficial to others and also to other religions, doing otherwise is harmful to one's own religion and to the religion of others. One who praises one's own religion out of excessive devotion, and condemns others with the thought that 'I One should glorify one's own religion', he only harms one's own religion... One should listen to and respect the principles laid down by others."

## 5. GOOD KARMA

"Devananapriya—beloved of the gods, King Piyadasi, thus says: It is difficult to do good. He who does well first works hard. I have done many good things, and if my sons, grandsons, and their descendants do the same thing until the end of the world, they will also do a lot of good. But any one of them who ignores this, will do evil. Indeed, it is easy to do evil."

## 6. THE GIFT OF DHAMMA AND THE DHAMMA JOURNEY

"Devanam Priya-Beloved of the Gods, King Piyadasi, thus speaks: There is no gift equal to the gift of the Dhamma, (no acquaintance) acquaintance with the Dhamma, (no distribution like) the distribution of the Dhamma, and (no kinship ) like kinship through Dhamma. And this includes: proper behavior towards servants and employees, respect towards mother and father, generosity towards friends, companions, relatives, brahmins and ascetics, and non-killing of animals. Therefore, a father, a son, a brother, a teacher, a friend, a companion or a neighbor should say: "This is good, this must be done." One gains in this world and receives great merit in the next by giving the gift of the Dhamma."

"In ancient times, kings used to go on tours for fun, which included hunting and other entertainments. But ten years after the coronation of the Beloved of the Gods, he went on a tour of Sambodhi [the site of Buddha's enlightenment] and thus founded Dhamma tourism. During these visits, the following things took place: visits and gifts to brahmins and sanyasis, gifts of gold and presents to elders, visits to people in the countryside, instructing them in the Dhamma, and discussing the Dhamma with them as appropriate. This is what pleases King Piyadasi, the beloved of the gods, and it is, as it were, another kind of revenue."


## 7. WELFARE OF PEOPLE


"Devanāma Priya—Beloved of the Gods, King Piyadasi, does not consider glory and fame to be of great account, so long as they are attained through my subjects respecting the Dhamma and practicing the Dhamma, both now and in the future . For this only, King Piyadasi, Devanam Priya—beloved of the gods, desires glory and fame. And whatever effort Piyadasi, the beloved king of the gods, is making is only for the welfare of the people in the other world, and there will be little evil in them. And being virtuous is inauspicious. It is difficult for a humble person or a noble person to do this, except with great effort, and to the exclusion of other interests. In fact, it may be even more difficult for a great person to do so."

"Everywhere, within the Beloved of the Gods, within the domain of King Piyadasi, and among people beyond the limits... Everywhere Devnam Beloved-Beloved of the Gods, King Piyadasi has made provision for two types of medical treatment: Medical treatment For humans and animals..."

"I got wells dug and trees planted along the roads for the benefit of humans and animals."

"Devanāma Priya—Beloved of the Gods, King Piyadasi, says thus: In the past, the business of the kingdom was not transacted nor reported to the king at all times. But now I have ordered that at any time I am eating, whether in the women's quarters, in the bedroom, in the chariot, in the palanquin, in the park, or wherever, reporters should be posted to give this instruction that they report. Me for the affairs of the people so that wherever I am I can be involved in these matters."

## 1.14 SPEECHDELIVERED TO THE CONSTITUENT ASSEMBLY ON AUGUST 14, 1947 MIDNIGHT, BY JAWAHARLAL NEHRUH TITLED 'TRYST WITH DESTINY'

(JawaharlalNehru (1889-1964) –Independent India's first Prime Minister gave famous speech on the midnight of

14ᵗʰ August 1947 in Parliament house. This is the excerpt
of the speech known as "TRYST WITH DESTINY")

"Long years ago, we made a tryst with destiny,
and now the time comes when we shall redeem our pledge,
not wholly or in full measure, but very substantially.

At the stroke of the midnight hour, when the
world sleeps, India will awake to life and freedom. A
moment comes, which comes but rarely in history, when
we step out from the old to the new, when an age ends,
and when the soul of a nation, long suppressed, finds
utterance.

It is fitting that at this solemn moment, we take
the pledge of dedication to the service of India and her
people and to the still larger cause of humanity.

At the dawn of history, India started on her
unending quest, and trackless centuries are filled with her
striving and grandeur of her success and failures. Through
good and ill fortune alike, she has never lost sight of that
quest, forgotten the ideals which gave her strength. We
end today a period of misfortunes and India discovers
herself again.

The achievement we celebrate today is but a step,
an opening of opportunity to the greater triumphs and
achievements that await us. Are we brave enough and
wise enough to grasp this opportunity and accept the
challenge of the future?

Freedom and power bring responsibility. The
responsibility rests upon this Assembly, a sovereign body
representing the sovereign people of India. Before the
birth of freedom, we have endured all the pains of labor

and our hearts are heavy with the memory of this sorrow. Some of those pains continue even now. Nevertheless, the past is over and it is the future that beckons us now.

That future is not one of ease or resting but of incessant striving so that we may fulfill the pledges we have so often taken and the one we shall take today. The service of India means, the service of the millions who suffer. It means the ending of poverty and ignorance and poverty and disease and inequality of opportunity.

The ambition of the greatest men of our generation has been to wipe every tear from every eye. That may be beyond us, but as long as there are tears and suffering, so long our work will not be over.

And so, we have to labor and to work, and to work hard, to give reality to our dreams. Those dreams are for India, but they are also for the world, for all the nations and peoples are too closely knit together today for any one of them to imagine that it can live apart.

Peace is said to be indivisible, so is freedom, so is prosperity now, and also is disaster in this one world that can no longer be split into isolated fragments.

To the people of India, whose representatives we are, we make an appeal to join us with faith and confidence in this great adventure. This is no time for petty and destructive criticism, no time for ill will or blaming others. We have to build the noble mansion of free India where all her children may dwell.

The appointed day has come -the day appointed by destiny- and India stands forth again, after long slumber and struggle, awake, vital, free and independent.

The past clings on to us still in some measure and we have to do much before we redeem the pledges we have so often taken. Yet the turning-point is past, and history begins anew for us, the history which we shall live and act and others will write about.

It is a fateful moment for us in India, for all Asia and for the world. A new star rises, the star of freedom in the East, a new hope comes into being, a vision long cherished materializes. May the star never set and that hope never be betrayed!

We rejoice in that freedom, even though clouds surround us, and many of our people are sorrow stricken and difficult problems encompass us. But freedom brings responsibilities and burdens and we have to face them in the spirit of a free and disciplined people.

On this day our first thoughts go to the architect of this freedom, the Father of our Nation, who, embodying the old spirit of India, held aloft the torch of freedom and lighted up the darkness that surrounded us.

We have often been unworthy followers of his and have strayed from his message, but not only we but succeeding generations will remember this message and bear the imprint in their hearts of this great son of India, magnificent in his faith and strength and courage and humility. We shall never allow that torch of freedom to be blown out, however high the wind or stormy the tempest.

Our next thoughts must be of the unknown volunteers and soldiers of freedom who, without praise or reward, have served India even unto death.

We think also of our brothers and sisters who have been cut off from us by political boundaries and who unhappily cannot share at present in the freedom that has come. They are of us and will remain of us whatever may happen, and we shall be sharers in their good [or] ill fortune alike.

The future beckons to us. Whither do we go and what shall be our Endeavour? To bring freedom and opportunity to the common man, to the peasants and workers of India; to fight and end poverty and ignorance and disease; to build up a prosperous, democratic and progressive nation, and to create social, economic and political institutions which will ensure justice and fullness of life to every man and woman.

We have hard work ahead. There is no resting for any one of us till we redeem our pledge in full, till we make all the people of India what destiny intended them to be.

We are citizens of a great country on the verge of bold advance, and we have to live up to that high standard. All of us, to whatever religion we may belong, are equally the children of India with equal rights, privileges and obligations. We cannot encourage communalism or narrow-mindedness, for no nation can be great whose people are narrow in thought or in action.

To the nations and peoples of the world we send greetings and pledge ourselves to cooperate with them in furthering peace, freedom and democracy.

And to India, our much-loved motherland, the ancient, the eternal and the ever-new, we pay our reverent homage and we bind ourselves afresh to her service. Jai Hind."

## 1.15 INSCRIPTION AT THE STATUE OF UNITY –(STATUE OF SARDAR VALLABHBHAI PATEL ) AT EKTA NAGAR (KEVADIYA-GUJARAT)

(Note -The exact script at the site of the inscription may slightly vary – here a translation is given for information purpose- Any error apoliged in this regard )

**HINDI-एक भारत श्रेष्ठ भारत**

**ENGLISH- ONE INDIA GREAT INDIA**

Twenty two scheduled Indian Languages

Hindi - एक भारत श्रेष्ठ भारत

Assamese –ৱান ইণ্ডিয়া গ্ৰেটে ইণ্ডিয়া

Bengali-এক ভারত মহান ভারত

Bodo-दरसे भारतसाबसिन भारत

Dogri- एक भारत श्रेष्ठ भारत

Gujarati–એક ભારત શ્રેષ્ઠ ભારત

Kannada-ಏಕ ಭಾರತ ಶ್ರೇಷ್ಠ ಭಾರತ

Kashmiri- एक भारत श्रेष्ठ भारत
ہِندُستان چھِس ہِندُستانَاَکھ

Konkani- एक भारत श्रेष्ठ भारत

Maithili- एक भारत श्रेष्ठ भारत

Malayalam-വൺ ഇന്ത്യ എക്സലന്റ് ഇന്ത്യ

Manipuri-

ꯑꯃ ꯚꯥꯔꯇ ꯑꯦꯛꯁꯦꯂꯦꯟꯇ ꯚꯥꯔꯇ॥

Marathi-एक भारत श्रेष्ठ भारत

Nepali- एक भारत श्रेष्ठ भारत

Odia-ଗୋଟିଏ ଭାରତ ଉତ୍କୃଷ୍ଟ ଭାରତ।

Punjabi- ਇੱਕ ਭਾਰਤ ਉੱਤਮ ਭਾਰਤ

Sanskrit –एकं भारतं श्रेष्ठ भारत

Santali- मित् भारत सोरास भारत

Sindhi-هڪ هندستان بهتري ن

Tamil-ஒன்இந்தியாஎக்ஸலண்ட்இந்தியா

Telugu-వన్ ఇండియా ఎక్ సలంట్ ఇండియా

Urdu- ایک ہندوستان بہترین ہندوستان

## Six International Languages Recognised by United Nations Organisation

Arabic -الهند الواحدة الهند العظمى

Chinese – 一印度大印度

English -One India Great India

French –Une Indela  GrandeInde

Russian –ОднаИндия, ВеликаяИндия

Spanish - Una India Gran India

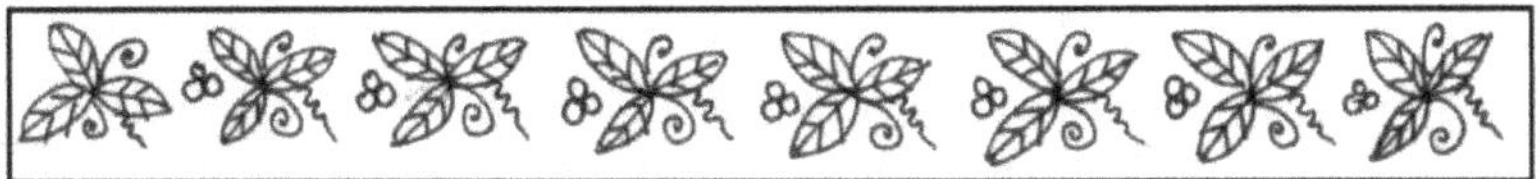

# CHAPTER-2 : QUOTATIONS BY GREAT LEADERS OF OUR NATION

## (1) CHANAKYA

"Love or affection towards an individual or nation, is indicated by good actionsnot merely be words. The adoration towards nation is expressed by works of welfare equally done by the ruler and theruled. The ruler himself must be engaged, in welfare of the country and also should select officials examining their involvement with the public good. Self-centered people greedy of the power should be kept away"

***

"If one limb of the body is defected or inflicted with, disease, the whole feels thepain. Same way if any department, minister or official of the state is faulty, the whole country is affected. An administrator should try hard to curb it."

***

"It is impossible to know when and how much water a fish drank, similar is the act of stealing government money by officials."

***

"To increase the wealth of the nation, a king should keep knowledge of history, traditions and trade practices,thieves"

***

"प्रजासुखे सुखं राज्ञ: प्रजानां च हिते हितम् ।<br>नात्मप्रियं हितं राज्ञ: प्रजानां तु प्रियं हितम् ।।

"Prajasukhesukhamrajya: Prajaana cha hitehitam.

NatmapriyaHitam Rajya: Prajanan Tu Priya Hitam."

"Peoples happiness should be King's happiness. Welfare of people is King's welfare. For a king, there is no task which is only individualistic and pleasurable to him only. It is king's utmost duty to look after progress and welfare of people of his country."

***

"तस्मान्तित्योत्थितो राजा कुर्यादिर्थानुशासनम् ।<br>अर्थस्य मूलमुत्थानमनर्थस्य विपर्यय: ।।"

"Tasmantityotthito Raja Kuryadarthanushasanam.

ArthasyaMoolmutthanmanarthasyaViparyayah."

"Therefore the king should rise up and discipline his wealth The root of wealth is the rise of evil and the opposite of evil."

**-Chanakya** ( 375–283 BCE) was an ancient Indian polymath who was active as a teacher, author,

102

strategist, philosopher, economist, jurist,     and     royal advisor

## (2) MAHARANA PRATAP

"Until I free my holy motherland from the enemies, I will neither live in palaces, nor sleep on a bed, nor eat food in gold, silver or any metal vessel. The shade of the trees will be my palace, the grass will be my bed and the leaves will be my food."

–**Maharana Pratap (Pratap singh)** (1540-1597)An Indian warrior  king  of Mewar from the Sisodia Dynesty

## (3) CHHATRAPATI SHIVAJI MAHARAJ

"First Nation, then guru, then parents then God, so first one should not look at himself but at nation"

***

"Freedom is a blessing, that every one is entitled to get"

***

"No matter how strong the enemy is.He can also be defeated by our intentions and enthusiasm alone"

-**Chhatrapati Shivaji Maharaj**- Shivaji- I -(Shivaji Bhonsle)(1630 – 1680 ) An  Indian warrior king , and A founder of Maratha dynasty

## (4) RANI LAXMIBAI OF JHANSI

"I shall not surrender my Jhansi."

***

"If defeated and killed on the field of battle, we shall surely earn eternal glory and salvation."

***

"We fight for independence. In the words of Lord Krishna we will, if we are victorious, enjoy the fruits of victory."

- **Rani Lakshmibai**, the **Rani of Jhansi** ( 1828 — 1858), was the Maharani of the princely state of Jhansi . Freedom fighter.

## (5) MAHATMA GANDHI

"No people have risen who thought only of rights. Only those did so who thought of duties."

***

"Violence becomes imperative when an attempt is made to assert rights without any reference to duties".

***

"Swaraj means ability to regard every inhabitant of India as our own brother or sister."

***

. "A nation's culture resides in the hearts and in the souls of its people."

***

"A small body of determined spirits fired by an unquenchable faith in their mission can alter the course of history".

***

"Greatness of a nation is judged by the way its animals are treated".

***

"Be the change you wish to see in others"

***

"In a gentle way, you can shake the world."

***

"The weak can never forgive. Forgiveness is the attribute of the strong."

***

"An eye for an eye only ends up making the whole world blind."

***

"You must not lose faith in humanity. Humanity is an ocean; if a few drops of the ocean are dirty, the ocean does not become dirty."

***

"See the good in people and help them."

***

"Live as if you were to die tomorrow. Learn as if you were to live forever."

***

"Where there is love there is life."

***

"The day the power of love overrules the love of power, the world will know peace."

***

"First they ignore you, then they laugh at you, then they fight you, then you win."

***

"It is better to be violent, if there is violence in our hearts, than to put on the cloak of nonviolence to cover impotence."

***

"Freedom is never dear at any price. It is the breath of life. What would a man not pay for living?"

***

"I am prepared to die, but there is no cause for which I am prepared to kill."

***

"Non-cooperation with evil is as much a duty as is cooperation with good."

***

"Power is of two kinds. One is obtained by the fear of punishment and the other by acts of love. Power based on love is a thousand times more effective and permanent then the one derived from fear of punishment."

***

"Non-violence is the greatest force at the disposal of mankind. It is mightier than the mightiest weapon of destruction devised by the ingenuity of man. Destruction is not the law of the humans. Man lives freely only by his readiness to die, if need be, at the hands of his brother, never by killing him. Every murder or other injury, no matter for what cause, committed or inflicted on another is a crime against humanity."

**-Mahatma Gandhi- Mohandas Karamchand Gandhi** ( 1869 – 1948) considered as Father of Nation , An Indian lawyer, anti-colonial nationalist and political ethicist who employed nonviolent resistance to lead the successful campaign for India's independence from British rule. He inspired movements for civil rights and freedom across the world. His movements inspire Martin Luther king Jr. and Nelson Mandela  He was a martyr for non violence and truth.

## (6) SARDAR VALLABHBHAI PATEL

"Young men and women are to build-up a strong character. A nation's greatness was reflected in the character of her people. If it was sullied by selfishness, such a people could not prosper or achieve great things. Selfishness had its place in life as everyone had to look to his own needs and that of his family, but it could not be made the be – all and end – all of life."

***

"My only desire is that India should be a good producer and no one should be hungry, shedding tears for food in the country."

***

"Non-violence has to be observed in thought, word and deed. The measure of our non-violence will be the measure of our success."

***

"In a domestic Government unity and co-operation are essential requisites. "

***

"Today we must remove distinctions of high and low, rich and poor, caste or creed."

***

"Religion is a matter between the man and his Maker."

***

"Manpower without Unity is not a strength unless it is harmonized and united properly, then it becomes a spiritual power."

***

"No distinctions of caste and creed should hamper us. All are the sons and daughters of India. We should all love our country and build our destiny on mutual love and help."

***

"Every citizen of India must remember that he is an Indian and he has every right in this country but with certain duties."

***

"The negligence of a few could easily send a ship to the bottom, but it required the whole-hearted co-operation of all on board; she could be safely brought to port."

***

"Faith is of no avail in absence of strength. Faith and strength, both are essential to accomplish any great work."

***

"A war based on Satyagraha is always of two kinds. One is the war we wage against injustice and the other we fight against our own weaknesses."

***

"There is something unique in this soil, which despite many obstacles has always remained the abode of great souls."

***

"One can take the path of revolution but the revolution should not give a shock to the society. There is no place for violence in revolution."

***

"Ours is a non-violent war, It is Dharma yuddha."

***

"Two ways of building character – cultivating strength to challenge oppression, and tolerate the resultant hardships that give rise to courage and awareness."

***

"The main task before India today is to consolidate herself into a well-knit and united power…"

***

"It is the prime responsibility of every citizen to feel that his country is free and to defend its freedom is his duty."

***

"Even if we lose the wealth of thousands, and our life is sacrificed, we should keep smiling and be cheerful keeping our faith in God and Truth"

***

"By common endeavor we can raise the country to a new greatness, while a lack of unity will expose us to fresh calamities"

***

"Happiness and misery are paper balls. Don't be afraid of death. Join the nationalist forces, be united. Give work to those who are hungry, food to individuals, forget your quarrels."

***

"I am blunt and uncultured. To me there is only one answer to these questions. That answer is not that you should shut yourselves in colleges and learn history and mathematics while the country is on fire and everybody is fighting freedom's battle. Your place is by the side of your countrymen, who are fighting the freedom's battle."

***

"I am a man who has forgotten caste. The whole of Hindustan is my village, eighteen varnas-casts  are my brotherhood."

**-SardarVallabhbhai Jhaverbhai Patel** (1875 – 1950), commonly known as Sardar Patel, Iron Man Of India  ,  **was**   an Indian independence nationalist, influential lawyer, barrister and statesman who served as the  first Deputy  Prime  Minister and Home  Minister  of India

## (7) JAWAHARLAL NEHRU

"A moment comes, which comes but rarely in history when we step out from the old to the new, when an  age  ends,  and  when  the  soul  of  a  nation  long suppressed finds utterance."

***

"Citizenship consists in the service of the country."

***

"To awaken the people, it is the women who must be awakened. Once she is on the move, the family moves, the village moves, the nation moves."

***

"Democracy is good. I say this because other systems are worse."

***

"It is science alone that can solve the problems of hunger and poverty, of insanitation and illiteracy, of superstition and deadening custom and tradition, of vast resources running to waste, of a rich country inhabited by starving people."

***

"India has known the innocence and insouciance of childhood, the passion and abandon of youth, and the ripe wisdom of maturity that comes from long experience of pain and pleasure; and over and over a gain she has renewed her childhood and youth and age"

***

"The best and noblest gifts of humanity cannot be the monopoly of a particular race or country; its scope may not be limited nor may it be regarded as the miser's hoard buried underground."

***

"Fine buildings, fine pictures and books and everything that is beautiful are certainly signs of civilization. But an even better sign is a fine man who is unselfish and works with others for the good of all. To work together is better than to work singly, and to work together for the common good is best of all."

***

"Culture is the widening of the mind and of the spirit."

***

"Without peace, all other dreams vanish and are reduced to ashes."

***

"Citizenship consists in the service of the country."

***

"The only alternative to coexistence is destruction."

***

"Socialism is... not only a way of life, but a certain scientific approach to social and economic problems."

***

"A leader or a man of action in a crisis almost always acts subconsciously and then thinks of the reasons for his action."

**-Jawaharlal Nehru** (1889 – 1964) An Indian anti-colonial nationalist, secular humanist, social democrat and first prime minister of India.

## (8) NETAJI SUBHASCHANDRA BOSE

"Delhi Chalo "slogen of Indian National Army Given By Subhash Chandra Bose

Apart From that "Jai Hind" Slogan was also popular in Indian National Army.

***

"Tum MujheKhoon Do, Main Tumhe Azadi Dunga"

"Give me blood, and I will give you freedom."

***

"No real change in history can be achieved by discussions"

***

"We must have the courage to dare and endure."

***

"It is not necessary to wait for the permission of others to secure our rights."

***

"Freedom is not given, it is taken."

***

"We must fight if we want to live."

***

"One individual may die for an idea, but that idea will, after his death, incarnate itself in a thousand lives."

***

"The true source of rights is duty. If we all discharge our duties, rights will not be far to seek."

***

"The nation will not be satisfied with mere

political independence ."

***

"Courage, sacrifice, determination, commitment, toughness, heart, talent, guts. That's what little girls are made of."

***

"Victory or defeat is not important, but the fight itself is everything."

***

" Life loses half its interest if there isno struggle-if there are no risks to be taken"

***

"Never lose your faith in the destiny of India. There is no power on Earth that can keep India in bondage. India will be free, that too, soon."

***

"It is our duty to pay for our liberty with our own blood."

***

" Life loses half its interest if there is no struggle — if there are no risks to be taken."

***

"It is blood alone that can pay the price of freedom. Give me blood and I will give you freedom"

- **NetajiSubhas Chandra Bose** (1897 – 1945) Known as Netaji Subhas Chabdra Bose was an Indian nationalist and founder general of Azad Hind fauz

## (9) DR.BHIMRAO RAMJI AMBEDKAR

"Democracy is not merely a form of Government. It is primarily a mode of associated living, of conjoint communicated experience. It is essentially an attitude of respect and reverence towards our fellow men".

***

"I like the religion that teaches liberty, equality, and
fraternity."

***

"Cultivation of mind should be the ultimate aim of
humane existence."

***

"A great man is different from an eminent one in that
he is ready to be the servant of the society."

***

"Freedom of mind is the real freedom."

***

"I am proud of my country, India, for having
a constitution that enshrines principles of democracy,
socialism, and secularism."

***

"Law and order are the medicine of the body
politic, and when the body politic gets sick, medicine
must be administered."

***

"I measure the progress of a community by the degree
of progress which women have achieved."

***

"Freedom of mind is the real freedom.
A person whose mind is not free though he may not be in
chains, is a slave,not a free man.One whose mind is not
free, though he may not be in prison, is a prisoner and not

a free man.One whose mind is not free though alive, is no
better than dead.Freedom of mind is the proof of one's
existence."

***

"Equality may be a fiction but nonetheless one must
accept it as a governing principle."

***

"Justice has always evoked ideas of equality, of
proportion of compensation.Equity signifies equality.
Rules and regulations, right and righteousness are
concerned with equality in value. If all men are equal,
then all men are of the same essence, and the common
essence entitles them of the same fundamental rights and
equal liberty..."

***

"In short justice is another name of liberty, equality and
fraternity."

***

"Be Educated, Be Organised and Be Agitated"

***

"So long as you do not achieve social liberty, whatever
freedom is provided by the law is of no avail to you."

***

"We are Indians, firstly and lastly."

-Dr. **Bhimrao Ramji Ambedkar** (1891 – 1956)Known as Architect Of Indian Constitution ,  was an Indian jurist, economist, social reformer and political leader who headed the committee drafting the Constitution of India , served as Law and Justice minister

## (10) BAL GANGADHAR TILAK

"Swaraj is my birthright, and I shall have it!"

***

"If we trace the history of any nation backwards into the past, we come at last to a period of myths and traditions which eventually fade away into impenetrable darkness."

-**Bal Gangadhar Tilak** ( 1856 – 1920), also known as Lokmanya Tilak  was an Indian nationalist, teacher, and an independence activist. He was one third of the Lal Bal Pal triumvirate

## (11) VEER SAVARKAR

"Our Motherland Sacrifice for you is like life Living without you is death."

***

"Loyalty to duty consists only in facing difficulties, suffering and struggling throughout life. Fame and failure are just matters of chance."

***

"The silent prayer made to the Lord for the freedom of our country, nation, society is also the biggest sign of non-violence."

***

"Suffering is the only power that tests a person on the test and makes him move forward."

***

"No one attains death before the time and when the time comes, no one can escape it. Thousands and lakhs die of disease, but for those who die in the dharm - yuddh , it is a matter of great fortune. Such people are pure souls."

***

"The root of all the power of a man is present in his own feeling."

-**Vinayak Damodar Savarkar** ( 1883 – 1966), was an Indian politician, activist, and writer. He spent 10 years 1911-1923 in Kalapani – imprisonment in cellular jail at Andaman from 1910 to1921. He was in Ratnagiri Jail from 1921 to 1924 and he was in house arrest from 1924 to 1937 inRatnagiri. He spent almost 27 years in Jail /House Arrest, out of which 10 years kalapani.

## (12) SWAMI VIVEKANANDA

"May He who is the Brahman of the Hindus, the Ahura-Mazda of the Zoroastrians, the Buddha of the Buddhists, the Jehovah of the Jews, the Father in Heaven of the Christians give strength to you to carry out your noble idea."

***

"The greatest religion is to be true to your own nature . Have faith in yourselves"

***

"The Vedanta recognizes no sin it only recognizes error. And the greatest error, says the Vedanta is to say that you are weak, that you are a sinner, a miserable creature, and that you have no power and you cannot do this and that."

***

"Arise! Awake! and stop not until the goal is reached"

***

"Proudly proclaim at the top of thy voice: "The Indian is my brother, the Indian is my life, India's gods and goddesses are my God. India's society is the cradle of my infancy, the pleasure-garden of my youth, the sacred heaven, the Varanasi of my old age."

***

"Every country under the sun, and our ideas will before long be a component of the many forces that are working to make up every nation in the world "

***

"Come, be men! Come out of your narrow holes and have a look abroad. See how nations are on the march! Do you love your country? Then come, let us struggle for higher and better things; look not back, no, not even if you see the dearest and nearest cry. Look not back, but forward!"

"Each nation has a main current in life in India it is religion. Make it strong and the waters on either side must move along with it."

***

"Here in India, it is religion that forms the very core of the national heart. It is the backbone, the bed-rock, the foundation upon which the national edifice has been built"

***

"Give up jealousy andconceit. Learn to work unitedly for others. This is the great need of our country "

***

"Every nation has a message to deliver, a mission to fulfill, a destiny to reach. The mission of India has been to guide humanity".

**-Swami Vivekananda** (1863-1902) An Indian Hindu monk, Philosopher,Oratorandauthor. He was disciple of Shri RamkrishnaParamhans. He has represented Hindu religion and world religious Congress Chicago and delivered his famous address on 11th September 1893. Thenafter Swamiji travelled throughout world and in India.

# (13) MAHARSHI ARVIND

***

"The existence of poverty is the proof of an unjust and ill-organised society, and our public charities are but the first tardy awakening in the conscience of a robber."

***

"The whole world yearns after freedom, yet each creature is in love with his chains; this is the first paradox and inextricable knot of our nature."

***

"War is a dangerous teacher and physical victory leads often to a moral defeat."

***

"Each religion has helped mankind. Paganism increased in man the light of beauty, the largeness and height of his life, his aim at a many-sided perfection; Christianity gave him some vision of divine love and charity; Buddhism has shown him a noble way to be wiser, gentler, purer, Judaism and Islam how to be religiously faithful in action and zealously devoted to God; Hinduism has opened to him the largest and profoundest spiritual possibilities."

***

"The Divine Truth is greater than any religion or creed or scripture or idea or philosophy."

***

"Our actual enemy is not any force exterior to ourselves, but our own crying weaknesses, our cowardice, our selfishness, our hypocrisy, our purblind sentimentalism."

***

"India saw from the beginning, and, even in her ages of reason and her age of increasing ignorance, she never lost hold of the insight, that life cannot be rightly seen in the sole light, cannot be perfectly lived in the sole power of its externalities."

**-AurobindoGhose-Maharshi** Arvind(1872 –1950) An Indian Philosopher ,yogi ,maharshi, poet,and Indiannationalist.He was also a journalist, editing newspapers such as VandeMataram. He joined the Indian movement for independence

## (14) RABINDRANATH TAGORE

"Where the mind is without fear and the head is held
high;
Where knowledge is free;
Where the world has not been broken up into fragments
by narrow domestic walls;
Where words come out from the depth of truth;
Where tireless striving stretches its arms toward
perfection;
Where the clear stream of reason has not lost its way into
the dreary desert sand of dead habit;
Where the mind is led forward by thee into ever-widening
thought and action -
Into that heaven of freedom, my Father, let my country
awake."

***

"The highest education is that which does not merely give us information but makes our life in harmony with all existence."

***

"We gain freedom when we have paid the full price."

***

"The one who plants trees, knowing that he will never sit in their shade, has at least started to understand the meaning of life"

***

"Patriotism cannot be our final spiritual shelter; my refuge is humanity. I will not buy glass for the price of diamonds, and I will never allow patriotism to triumph over humanity as long as I live."

— **Rabindranath Tagore** (1861 – 1941) A Bengali polymath who worked as a poet, writer, playwright, composer, philosopher, social reformer and painter. Also Known as Gurudev

## (15) LAL BAHADUR SHASTRI

"Discipline and united action are the real source of strength for the nation."

***

"Our country has often stood like a solid rock in the face of common danger, and there is a deep underlying unity which runs like a golden thread through all our seeming diversity."

***

"Jai Jawan Jai kishan"

***

"We believe in peace and peaceful development, not only for ourselves but for people all over the world."

- **Lal Bahadur Shastri ( 1904 – 1966)** An Indian politician and statesman who served as the 2nd Prime Minister of India . He promoted the Green and White Revolution in India.

## (16) INDIRA GANDHI

"There are moments in history when brooding tragedy and its dark shadows can be lightened by recalling great moments of the past – "

***

"People tend to forget their duties but remember their rights."

***

"Martyrdom does not end something; it is only a beginning."
***
"The power to question is the basis of all humane progress."

***

"Winning or losing of the election is less important than strengthening the country."

***

"All the people who fought for freedom were my heroes. I mean, that was the sort of story I liked reading freedom struggles and so on."

***

"A nation' s strength ultimately consists in what it can do on its own, and not in what it can borrow from others."

***

**-        Indira    Gandhi (1917    –    1984),**Also referred    as    Priyadarshini,An    Indian    politician    and stateswoman    who    served    as    the    third prime    minister    of India.

## (17) ATAL BIHARI VAJPAYEE

"I dream of an India that is prosperous, strong and caring. An India, that regains a place of honour in the comity of great nations."

***

"Empowering the individual means empowering the nation. And empowerment is best served through rapid economic growth with rapid social change."

***

"Jai Jawan Jai Kishan Jai Vigyaan"

"Indian democracy's greatest strength is that we have always put the nation above politics."

**-Atal Bihari Vajpayee ( 1924 – 2018)**An Indian politician who served three terms as the 10th Prime Minister of India,

## (18) DR. A.P.J. ABDUL KALAM

"As a young citizen of India, armed with technology and love for my nation, I realize, a small aim is a crime".

***

"We should not give up and we should not allow the problem to defeat us."

***

"The purpose of education is to make good human beings with skill and expertise... Enlightened human beings can be created by teachers."

***

"Unless India stands up to the world, no one will respect us. In this world, fear has no place. Only strength respects strength."

***

"Where do the evils like corruption arise from? It comes from the never-ending greed. The fight for corruption-free ethical society will have to be fought against this greed and replace it with 'what can I give' spirit."

*******

"Almost half of the population of the world lives in rural regions and mostly in a state of poverty. Such inequalities in humane development have been one of the primary reasons for unrest and, in some parts of the world, even violence."

*******

"Where there is righteousness in the heart, there is beauty in the character. When there is beauty in the character, there is harmony in the home. When there is harmony in the home, there is order in the nation. When there is order in the nation, there is peace in the world."

*******

"If a country is to be corruption free and become a nation of beautiful minds, I strongly feel there are three key societal members who can make a difference. They are the father, the mother and the teacher."

*******

**-AvulPakirJainulabdeen Abdul Kalam (** 1931-2015) An Indian aerospace scientist and statesman who served as the 11th president of India .

## (19) NARENDAR DAMODARDAS MODI

"We want to make nation-building a people's movement."

***

"Let the professionals like doctors & engineers teach in schools once a week. Let's make teaching a national movement necessary for Nation building."

**-Narendra Damodardas Modi** (Born 1950) An Indian leader- politician who became prime minister of India- from a humble famiy back ground from small town of Vadnagar Gujarat . He was earlier Chief Minister of State of Gujarat.

# CHAPTER-3: NATION AND QUOTATIONS ON NATION

## 3.1 HOW A NATION IS BORN

***

### 3.1  DAVID BEN GURION

"A nation is neither given as a gift, nor got as a present nor bought with gold or silver, nor offered by a treaty, nor achieved by an agreement. It is the creation of the people , the people who identify themselves with the soil , where they work ,where they suffer, where they toil , shedding their sweats, shedding their blood ,shedding their tears , not for a day or two but from generations up to generations , that is how a nation is born"

–        **David  Ben  Gurion** (1886-1973)First  Prime Minister Of Israel

# 3.2 QUOTATIONS ON NATION BY GIUSEPPE MAZZINNI

## 3.2 GIUSEPPE MAZZINNI

***

"God has given you your country as cradle ,and humanity as mother ,you cannot rightly love your brethren of the cradle if you love not the common mother"

***

"O my Brothers! love your country . Our country is our home , the home which 'god has given us , placing therein a numerous family which we love and are loved by ,  and with which we have a  more intimate and quicker communion of feeling and thought than with others ; a family which by its concentration upon a given spot , and by the homogeneous nature of its elements , is destined for a special kind of activity ."

***

"Love your country .your country is the land where your parents sleep, where is spoken that  language in which chosen of your heart ,blushing ,whispered the first word of love ; it is home that God has given you that by striving to perfect yourselves therein you may prepare to ascend to him "

***

"A country is not mere territory, the particular territory is only its foundation .The country is the idea which rises upon that foundation. It is the sentiment of love, the sense of fellowship which binds together all the sons of that territory "

***

"Every nation is destined, by the law of God and humanity, to form a free and equal community of brothers "

***

"Humanity is the association of peoples; it is the alliance of peoples in order to work out their missions in peace and love. To forget humanity is to suppress the aim of our labors, to cancel the nation is to suppress the instrument by which to achieve the aim "

***

"Every nation has its mission, which is to serve the progress and civilization of humanity at large."

***

"The religion of humanity is love."

***

"Ideas grow quickly when watered by the blood of martyrs."

***

"The honor of a country depends much more on removing its faults than on boasting of its qualities."

***

"Every nation is destined, by the law of God and humanity, to form a free and equal community of brothers."

****

"Without country you have neither name, token, voice, nor rights, no admission as brothers into the fellowship of the people. You are the bastards of humanity. Soldiers without a banner, Israelites among the nations, you will find neither faith nor protection; none will be sureties for you. Do not beguile yourselves with the hope of emancipation from unjust social conditions if you do not first conquer a country for yourselves."

****

"Nations, like individuals, live and die; but civilization cannot die."

****

"No nation deserves freedom or can long retain it which does not win it for itself. Revolutions must be made by the people and for the people."

****

"Liberty and equality – lovely and sacred words!"

****

"So long as a single one amongst your brothers has no vote to represent him in the development of the national life, so long as a single man, able and willing to work, languishes in poverty through want of work to do, you have no country in the sense in which country ought to exist-the country of all and for all."

***

"Onesole God;
One sole ruler, — his Law;
One sole interpreter of that law — Humanity."

***

"The religion of humanity is love."

***

"No nation deserves freedom or can long retain it which does not win it for itself. Revolutions must be made by the people and for the people.

***

"A nation isthe universality of citizens speaking the same tongue."

***

"Great revolutions are the work rather of principles than of bayonets, and are achieved first in the moral, and afterwards in the material sphere."

***

"The great men of the earth are but the marking-stones on the road of humanity; they are the priests of its religion."

***

"Insurrection by means of guerrilla bands is the true method of warfare for all nations desirous of emancipating themselves from a foreign yoke. It is invincible, indestructible."

***

"The honor of a country depends much more on removing its faults than on boasting of its qualities."

***

"The republic, as I at least understand it, means association, of which liberty is only an element, a necessary antecedent. It means association, a new philosophy of life, a divine Ideal that shall move the world, the only means of regeneration vouchsafed to the human race."

***

"Liberty, understood by materialists as the right to do or not to do anything not directly injurious to others, we understand as the faculty of choosing, among the various modes of fulfilling duty, those most in harmony with our own tendencies."

–**Giuseppe Mazzini** (1805-1872)Italian Politician, Journalist and activist for the unification of Italy and spearheaded Italian revolutionary movement and. His efforts helped bring about the independent and unified Italy.Nick named Beating Heart of Italy

## 3.3 QUOTATIONS ON NATION BY VARIOUS SCHOLERS

### 3.3 (1) THEODORE ROOSVELT

"No nation can be really great unless it is great in peace, in industry, integrity, honesty. Skilled intelligence in civic affairs and industrial enterprises alike; the special ability of the artist, the man of letters, the man of science, and the man of business; the rigid determination to wrong no man, and to stand for righteousness-all these are necessary in a great nation."

**-Theodore Roosevelt** (1858-1919) An American. American politician, statesman, soldier, conservationist, naturalist, historian, and writer who served as the 26th president of the United States .

### 3.3 (2) NAPOLEON BONAPARTE

"It is in times of difficulty that great nations like great men display the whole energy of their character and become an object of admiration to posterity."

**–Napoleon Bonaparte(1769-1821)** A great French military commander , political leader and Emperor of the France.

### 3.3 (3) JOHN RUSKIN

"Great nations write their autobiographies in three manuscripts, the book of their deeds, the book of their words and the book of their art. Not one of these books can be understood unless we read the two others, but of the three the only trustworthy one is the last."

**-John Ruskin** (1819-1900) An English Writer, Philosopher, and polymath

### 3.3 (4) LAO TZU

"A great nation is like a great man:
When he makes a mistake, he realizes it.
Having realized it, he admits it.
Having admitted it, he corrects it.
He considers those who point out his faults
as his most benevolent teachers.
He thinks of his enemy
as the shadow that he himself casts."

***

"Governing a great nation is like cooking a small fish -
too much handling will spoil it."

**–Lao Tzu**,( 6th century BC)  An Ancient Taoist
Chinese
philosopher

### 3.3 (5) JOHN F. KENNEDY

"Ask not what your country can do for you...ask what
you can do for your country."

***

"All this will not be finished in the first one
hundred days. Nor will it be finished in the first one
thousand days, not in the life of this Administration, nor

even perhaps in our lifetime on this planet. But let us begin."

***

"A nation that is afraid to let its people judge the truth and falsehood in an open market is a nation that is afraid of its people. Let us never negotiate out of fear. But let us never fear to negotiate."

***

"A man may die, nations may rise and fall, but an idea lives on."

***

"A nation reveals itself not only by the men it produces but also by the men it honors, the men it remembers."

**-John F. Kennedy**(1917-1963) An American Politician Served as 35th President Of United States Of America .

### 3.3 (6) ABRAHAM LINCOLN

"A nation that does not honor its heroes will not long endure."

- **Abraham Lincoln**( 1809 – 1865) An American

lawyer, politician, and statesman who served as the 16th president of the United States

## 3.3 (7) SIR WINSTON CHURCHILL

"A nation that fails to honor its heroes, soon will have no heroes to honor."

***

"A nation that doesn't honour its past has no future"

***

"A nation that forgets its past has no future"

**-Sir Winston Leonard Spencer Churchill**((1874 – 1965)  A British statesman, soldier, and writer who served as Prime Minister of the United Kingdom twice,

## 3.3 (8) KHALIL GIBRAN

"Pity the nation that is full of beliefs and empty of religion.
Pity the nation that wears a cloth it does not weave and eats a bread it does not harvest.

Pity the nation that acclaims the bully as hero, and that deems the glittering conqueror bountiful.

Pity a nation that despises a passion in its dream, yet submits in its awakening.

Pity the nation that raises not its voice
save when it walks in a funeral,
boasts not except among its ruins,
and will rebel not save when its neck is laid
between the sword and the block.

Pity the nation whose statesman is a fox,
whose philosopher is a juggler,
and whose art is the art of patching and mimicking

Pity the nation that welcomes its new ruler with
trumpeting,
and farewells him with hooting,
only to welcome another with trumpeting again.

Pity the nation whose sages are dumb with years
and whose strongmen are yet in the cradle.

Pity the nation divided into fragments,
each fragment deeming itself a nation."

**- Khalil Gibran** ( 1883 – 1931), A Labenes-American writer, poet and visual artist; (from the The Garden of The Prophet)

### 3.3 (9) CHARLES CALEB COLTON

"Liberty will not descend to a people, a people must raise themselves to liberty; it is a blessing that must be earned before it can be enjoyed."

**-Charles Caleb Colton** (1777 – 1832) An English cleric, writer and collector

### 3.3 (10) BENJAMIN FRANKLIN

"They that give up essential liberty to obtain a little temporary safety deserve neither liberty nor safety."

-**Benjamin Franklin(** 1706- 1790) An American polymath who was active as a writer, scientist, inventor, statesman, diplomat, printer, publisher, and political philosopher.

### 3.3 (11) WILLIAM JEFFERSON CLINTON

" When citizens are united there's no wrong that can not be fixed "

-**William Jefferson Clinton** ( born 1946) An American politician who served as the 42nd president of the United States.

### 3.3 (12) SOEKARNO

"Great nation is a nation that respects the services of the hero"

-**Sukarno or Soekarno** (1901 –1970)
AnIndonesian statesman, orator, revolutionary,and natio nalist  who was the first president of Indonesia.

### 3.3 (13) RALPH WALDO EMERSON

"Not gold but only men can make
A people great and strong;
Men who for truth and honor's sake
Stand fast and suffer long.

Brave men who work while others sleep,
Who dare while others fly—
They build a nation's pillars deep
And lift them to the sky."

**-Ralph Waldo Emerson** (1803 – 1882) who went by his middle name Waldo, An American essayist, lecturer, philosopher, abolitionist, and poet who led the transcendentalist movement.

### 3.3 (14) AUTHOR UNKNOWN ATTRIBUTED TO BENJAMIN DISRAELI

"Great nations rise and fall. The people go from bondage to spiritual truth, to great courage, from courage to liberty, from liberty to abundance, from abundance to selfishness, from selfishness to complacency, from complacency to apathy, from apathy to dependence, from dependence back again to bondage."

-Author unknown. Attributed to **Benjamin Disraeli,** ( 1804 – 1881) was a British statesman, Conservative politician, and writer who twice served as Prime Minister of the United Kingdom.

## 3.3 (15) AUTHOR UNKNOWN, "THREE THINGS"

"I know three things must always be
To keep a nation strong and free.
One is a hearthstone bright and dear,
With busy, happy loved ones near.
One is a ready heart and hand
To love, and serve, and keep the land.
is a worn and beaten way
where the people go to pray.
long as these are kept alive,
Nation and people will survive.
God keep them always, everywhere—
The home, the heart, the place of prayer."

-Author unknown, "Three Things", Sourcebook of Poetry (1968), comp. Al Bryant, . A variation of this poem appeared in the Congressional Record in 1959.

## 3.3 (16) CONFUCIUS

"When (a ruler) issues his notices and gives forth his orders, and the people are pleased, we have what may be called the condition of harmony. When superiors and inferiors love one another, we have the condition of benevolence. When the people get what they desire without seeking for it, we have the condition of confidence. When all things in the operations of heaven and earth that might be injurious are taken out of the way, we have the condition of rightness. Rightness and confidence, harmony and benevolence are the instruments of the presiding chieftain and the king. If anyone wishes to govern the people, and does not employ these instruments, he will not be successful."

"The strength of a nation derives from the integrity of the home."

- **Confucius** (c. 551 – c. 479 BCE) A Chinese religious preacher, philosopher and politician.

## 3.3 (17) JOSÉ PROTASIO RIZAL MERCADO Y ALONSO REALONDA

"I have observed that the prosperity or misery of each people is in direct proportion to its liberties or its prejudices and, accordingly, to the sacrifices or the selfishness of its forefathers. -Juan Crisostomo Ibarra"

— **José Protasio Rizal Mercadoy Alonso Realonda** (1861 – 1896) was a Filipino nationalist, writer and polymath.

## 3.3 (18) ELMER HOLMES DAVIS

"This nation will remain the land of the free only so long as it is the home of the brave."

-**Elmer Holmes Davis** (, 1890 – , 1958) An American news reporter, author, the Director of the United States Office of War Information during World War II .

## 3.3 (19) CALVIN COOLIDGE

"The nation which forgets its defenders will be itself forgotten."

**-Calvin Coolidge** (1872 – 1933) An American attorney and politician who served as the 30th president of the United States from 1923 to 1929.

### 3.3 (20) WILLIAM SOMERSET MAUGHAM

"If a nation values anything more than freedom, it will lose its freedom, and the irony of it is that if it is comfort or money that it values more, it will lose that too."

**-William Somerset Maugham (** 1874 – 1965) An English write.

### 3.3 (21) FREDERICK DOUGLASS

"The life of the nation is secure only while the nation is honest, truthful, and virtuous."

**-Frederick Douglass (** 1817 –1895) An American social reformer, abolitionist, orator, writer, and statesman.

### 3.3 (22) ALEKSANDR ISAYEVICH SOLZHENITSYN

"Literature transmits incontrovertible condensed experience... from generation to generation. In this way literature becomes the living memory of a nation."

**-Aleksandr Isayevich Solzhenitsyn** (1918–2008)A Russian writer. A prominent Soviet dissident.

### 3.3 (23) HENRY DAVID THOREAU

"There will never be a really free and enlightened state until the state comes to recognize the individual as a higher and independent power, from which all its own power and authority are derived, and treats him accordingly."

-**Henry David Thoreau** (1817-1862) An American philosopher, poet and environmentalscientist.

### 3.3 (24) ALBERT EINSTEIN

"The state is made for man, not man for the state."

-**Albert Einstein** (1879 –1955) was a German-born theoretical physicist.

### 3.3 (25) BENJAMIN DISRAELI

"Great countries are those that produce great people."

-**Benjamin Disraeli,** (1804 – 1881) A British statesman.

### 3.3 (26) MARTIN LUTHER KING JR.

"Ultimately a great nation is a compassionate nation."

***

"Our lives begin to end the day we become silent about things that matter."

***

" To other countries , I may Go as a tourist, but to India ,I come as a  Pilgrim"

- **Martin Luther King, Jr.**(1929-1968) An American Baptist minister and Activist, leader of the Civil Right Movements.

### 3.3 (27) CATHERINETHE GREAT

"Power without a nation's confidence is nothing."

-**Catherinethe great** (1729 –1796) Most commonly known as **Catherine the Great**, An  empress of Russia.

### 3.3 (28) MARY ELIZABETH ALEXANDER HANFORD DOLE

"We are a great nation because we are a good people."

-**Mary Elizabeth Alexander Hanford Dole** (Born, 1936)An American attorney, author, and politician.

### 3.3 (29) JOAN RUTH BADER GINSBURG

"If we gave up our freedom as the price of security, we would no longer be the great nation that we are."

**-Joan Ruth Bader Ginsburg** ( 1933 – , 2020) An American lawyer and jurist .

## 3.3 (30) NELSON ROLIHLAHLA MANDELA

"We understand it still that there is no easy road to freedom. We know it well that none of us acting alone can achieve success. We must therefore act together as a united people, for national reconciliation, for nation building, for the birth of a new world. Let there be justice for all. Let there be peace for all. Let there be work, bread, water and salt for all. Never, never and never again shall it be that this beautiful land will again experience the oppression of one by another and suffer the indignity of being the skunk of the world. Let freedom reign."

***

"The message of reconciliation, of nation-building, of granting amnesty, indemnity, has struck a powerful, favorable chord. And people can understand that we're here not for purposes of retribution but to forget the past and to build our country."

**-Nelson Rolihlahla Mandela** ( 1918 –  2013) A South African anti-apartheid activist and politician who served as the first president of South Africa.

## 3.3 (31) WILL DURANT

"A great civilization is not conquered from without until it has destroyed itself within."

***

"Civilization begins with order, grows with liberty,
and dies with chaos."

***

"From barbarism to civilization requires a
century; from civilization to barbarism needs but a day."

***

"So I should say that civilizations begin with
religion and stoicism: they end with scepticism and
unbelief, and the undisciplined pursuit of individual
pleasure. A civilization is born stoic and dies epicurean."

***

"The only real revolution is in the enlightenment
of the mind and the improvement of character, the only
real emancipation is individual, and the only real
revolutionaries are philosophers and saints."

***

"Those who know nothing about history are
doomed forever to repeat it."

***

"Rome remained great as long as she had enemies
who forced her to unity, vision, and heroism. When she
had overcome them all she flourished for a moment and
then began to die."

***

"The soul of a civilization is its religion, and it dies with its faith."

***

"Civilization is not inherited; it has to be learned and earned by each generation anew; if the transmission should be interrupted for one century, civilization would die, and we should be savages again."

***

"The family is the nucleus of civilization."

***

"Civilizations come and go; they conquer the earth and crumble into dust; but faith survives every desolation."

***

"Civilization is the order and freedom is promoting cultural activity."

***

"The principle of democracy is freedom, the principle of war is discipline; each requires the absence of the other."
***

"The goal of democracy is not to make every man equal, but to make his access to opportunity more equal. The ideal is not to raise every man to power, but to give him access to each point of entry where his fitness and skill can be tested. In other words, the hope of democracy is to offer a level playing field to start and to let your talents carry you where they may."
***

"Without religion, it is very possible that the world would have been less moral. Yes, immorality and crime still persisted, but the forces of religion probably dampened their effects."

**-Will Durant** (1885-1981)AnAmerican Writer, Historian and Philosopher , Authored Story of Civilization  in a span of forty years ( 11 Volumes ) published from 1935 to 1975 after studying world History

### 3.3 (32) ATIFETE JAHJAGA

"A democracy must be built through open societies that share information. When there is information, there is enlightenment. When there is debate, there are solutions. When there is no sharing of power, no rule of law, no accountability, there is abuse, corruption, subjugation, and indignation."

- **AtifeteJahjaga**(born 1975) A Kosova Albanian politician who served as the third President of Kosovo

## 3.3 (33) ANONYMOUS

You cannot get rich, without encouraging frugality.
You cannot make the weak strong, by making
the strong weak.
You can't belittle a big man, by  flattering  a strong man.
You cannot help the servant, by condemning the master.
You cannot nurture fraternity, by encouraging classism.
You cannot  help poor by  destroying  the rich .
You cannot  enjoy peace by taking debts.
You cannot overcome difficulty by spending
more than you earn.
You cannot make a man characterful and fearless  by
curtailing  a man's freedom or self-reliance .
You cannot help others by doing yourself,
what they should do.
- **Anonymous**

( Some times this quotes is assigned to Abraham Lincoln ,but this is not authenticated . The original source is anonymous )

# CHAPTER-4 QUOTATIONS OF VARIOUS SCHOLARS ACROSS WORLD IN PRAISE AND ON GLORY OF INDIA

## 4 (1) SWAMI VIVEKANANDA

"This is the ancient land where wisdom made it home before it went in to any other country , the same India whose influx of spirituality is represented as it were , on the material plane by rolling rivers like oceans , where the eternal Himalayas rising tier above tier with their snow-caps , look as it were in to the mysteries of heaven. Here the same India whose soil has been trodden by the feet of the greatest sages that ever lived. Here first sprang the inquiries in to the nature of man and in to the internal world. Here first arose the doctrines of the immortality of the soul, the existence of a supervising God, and immanent God in nature and in man and here the highest ideals of religion and philosophy have attained their culminating points. This is the land from whence like the tidal waves, spirituality and philosophy have again and again rushed out and deluged the world, and this is the land from whence once more such tides must proceed in order to bring life and vigor in to the decaying races of mankind. It is the same India which has withstood the shocks of centuries of hundreds of foreign invasions, of hundreds of upheavals of manners and customs It is the same land which stands firmer than any rock in the world, with its undying vigor, indestructible life . Its life is of the same nature as the soul without beginning and without end , immortal and we are the children of such a country ."

**-Swami Vivekananda** (1863-1902)An Indian Hindu monk, Philosopher,Orator and author .He was disciple of Shri RamkrishnaParamhans.

## 4 (2) MARK  TWAIN

"This is indeed India ! The land of dreams and romance , of fabulous wealth and fabulous poverty,of splendor and rags, of palaces and hovels, of  famine and pestilence, of genii and giants and Aladdin lamps, of tigers and elephants, of  the cobra and jungle , the country of a hundred nations and a hundred tongues, of a thousand religions and two million gods, cradle of the human race, birth place of human speech , mother of history , grandmother of legend , great grandmother of traditions . Whose yesterday bears date with shouldering antiquities of the rest of the nations − the one sole country under the sun that is endowed with an imperishable interest for alien prince and alien peasant for lettered and ignorant , wise and fool, rich and poor , bond and free, the one land that all men desire to see and having seen once , by even a glimpse would not give that glimpse for the show of all the rest of the globe combined."

***

"India had the start of the whole world in the beginning of things. She had the first civilization; she had the first accumulation of material wealth; she was populous with deep thinkers and subtle intellects; she had mines, and woods, and a fruitful soil. It would seem as if she should have kept the lead, and should be to-day not the meek dependent of an alien master, but mistress of the world, and delivering law and command to every tribe and nation in it. But, in truth, there was never any possibility of such supremacy for her."


**-Samuel Langhorne Clemens** ( 1835 – , 1910) best known by his pen name Mark Twain, An American writer, humorist, entrepreneur, publisher, and lecturer.


## 4 (3) FRIEDRICH MAX MULLER


"If I were to look over the whole world to find out the country most richly endowed with all wealth, power and beauty that nature can bestow – in some parts a very paradise on earth – I should point to India. If I were asked under what sky the human mind has most fully developed some of its choicest gifts has most deeply pondered on the greatest problems of life and has found solutions to some of them which well deserve the attention even of those who have studied Plato and kant –I should point to India. And if I were to ask myself from what literature we here in Europe we who have been nurtured almost exclusively on the thoughts of Greeks and Romans, may draw that corrective which is most wanted in order to make our inner life more perfect, more comprehensive, more universal, in fact moretruly humane, a life not for this life only but a transfigured and eternal life – again I should point to India "

***

"There are many points of great interest to the student of language, in the long history of the speech [of India]; and it has been truly said that Sanskrit is to the science of language What mathematics is to astronomy."

– **Friedrich Max Muller**(1823-1900) A German philologist and Orientalist, Editor of Sacred books of East.( 50 Volumes )

### 4 (4) MARQUIS DE LAPLACE

"It is India that gave us the ingenious method of expressing all numbers of ten symbol receiving a value of position as well as an absolute value; a profound and important idea which appear, so simple to us now, that we ignore its true merits."

**-Marquis de Laplace**(1749-1827) A French scholar and polymath , whose work was important to the development of Engineering ,Mathematics,Statistics , Physics ,astronomy and philosophy.

### 4 (5) ALBERT EINSTEIN

"We owe a lot to the Indians ,who taught us how to count ,without which no worthwhile scientific discovery could have been made. "

— **Albert Einstein** (1879-1955) A German Theoreticalphysicist.

## 4 (6) ALFRED NORTH WHITEHEAD

"Vedanta is the most impressive metaphysics thehuman mind has conceived "

— **Alfred North Whitehead** , (1861-1947)A British mathematician, logician and philosopher.

## 4 (7) ERWIN SCHRODINGER

"There is no kind of framework within which we can find consciousness in the plural; this is simply something we construct because of the temporal plurality of individuals, but it is a false construction...The only solution to this conflict insofar as any is available to us at all lies in the ancient wisdom of the Upanishad."

***

"The multiplicity is only apparent. This is the doctrine of the Upanishads. And not of the Upanishads only. The mystical experience of the union with God regularly leads to this view, unless strong prejudices stand in the West."

***

"There is obviously only one alternative, namely the unification of minds or consciousness. Their multiplicity is only apparent in truth there is only one mind. This is the doctrine of the Upanishads. "

-**Erwin Schrodinger** (1887-1961) An Austrian- Irish Physicist worked on Quantum Mechanics.

## 4 (8) NIELS BOHR

" I go to the Upanishads to ask questions "

–**Niels    Bohr**(1885-1962)A    Danish    Physicist Worked on quantum mechanics.

## 4 (9) ARCHIBALD EDWARD GOUGH

"The Upanishads are the loftiest utterances of Indian Intelligence ... Whatever value the reader may assign to the ideas they represents they are the highest product of the ancient mind almost the only element of interest in Indian literature , which is at every stage relate with them to saturation "

-    **Archibald    Edward    Gough**    (1845-1915) Theological scholar of the University of oxford , Principal Banaras college , Professor of philosophy presidency college Calcutta . The author of philosophy of Upanishads  and Ancient Indian Metaphysics.

## 4 (10) WILL DURANT

"As flowing rivers disappear in the sea, losing their name and form, thus a wise man, freed from name and form, goes to the divine person who is beyond all." Such a theory of life and death will not please Western man, whose religion is as permeated with individualism as are his political and economic institutions. But it has satisfied the philosophical Hindu mind with astonishing continuity."

***

"India was the motherland of our race and Sanskrit the mother of Europe's language : she was the mother of our philosophy ; mother , through the Arabs , of much of our Mathematics ; mother , through the

Buddha , of the ideals embodied in Christianity ; mother through the village community , of self-government and democracy. Mother India is in many ways the mother of us all "

***

"Perhaps in return for conquest, arrogance and spoliation, India will teach us the tolerance and gentleness of mature mind, understanding spirit and a unifying, pacifying love for all living things (human beings)"

***

"The Upanishads are as old as Homer, and as modern as Kant."

- **Will Durant** (1885-1981)AnAmerican Writer, Historian and Philosopher , Authored Story of Civilization  in a span of forty years ( 11 Volumes ) published from 1935 to 1975 after studying world History.

### 4 (11 ) ROMAINE ROLLAND

"If there is one place on the face of earth where all the dreams of living men have found a home from the very earliest days when man began  the dream of existence , it is India !"

— **Romaine Rolland**    (1866-1944)A  French Dramatist, Novelist, Essayist, Art Historian and mystic

## 4 (12) LEO TOLSTOY

"India which is the nursery of the great faiths of the world "

-Leo Tolstoy (1828-1910) A Russian writer greatest author of all time .

## 4 (13) ARNOLD J. TOYNBEE

"It is already becoming clear that a chapter which had a Western beginning will have to have an Indian ending if it is not to end in self-destruction of the humanrace. At this supremely dangerous moment of human history, the only way of salvation is the ancient Indian - Hindu way . Here we have the attitude and spirit that can make it possible for the human race to grow together in to a single family."

– **Arnold J. Toynbee** (1889-1975) English Historian and philosopher of History, Author of "study of History " (12 Volumes )published from 1934 to 1961.

## 4 (14) WERNER KARL HEISENBERG

"After the conversations about Indian philosophy , some of the ideas of Quantum Physics that had seemed so crazy suddenly made much more sense "- Werner Karl Heisenberg (1901-1976) German Theoretical Physicist and one of the main pioneer of quantum mechanics."

-**Werner Karl Heisenberg** ( 1901 –1976) A German theoretical physicist and one of the main pioneers of the theory of quantum mechanics.

## 4 (15) SIR WILLIAM JONES

"The Sanskrit language, whatever be its antiquity, is of a wonderful structure; more perfect than the Greek, more copious than the Latin, and more exquisitely refined than either, yet bearing to both of them a stronger affinity, both in the roots of verbs and the forms of grammar, than could possibly have been produced by accident; so strong indeed, that no philologer could examine them all three, without believing them to have sprung from some common source, which, perhaps, no longer exists; there is a similar reason, though not quite so forcible, for supposing that both the Gothic and the Celtic, though blended with a very different idiom, had the same origin with the Sanskrit; and the old Persian might be added to the same family".

- **Sir William Jones**( 1746-1794) A British Philologist scholar of ancient India.

### 4 (16) WILLIAMS JAMES

" From the Vedas we learn a practical art of surgery ,medicine, music, house building under which mechanized art is included. They are encyclopedia of every aspect of life , culture , religion , science ,ethics, law, cosmology and meteorology "

— **William James**(1842-1910) An American philosopher ,historian and psychologist . he is known as "Father of American psychology.

### 4 (17) RALPH WALDO EMERSON

"In the great books of India , an empire spoke to us, nothing small and unworthy , but large , serene , consistent , the voice of an intelligence, which in another age and climate had pondered and thus disposed of the questions that exercise us. "

— **Ralph Waldo Emerson**( 1803-1882) An American essayist, lecturer, philosopher and poet who led the transcendentalist  movement.

## 4 (18) HENRY DAVID THOREAU

"In the morning I bathe my intellect in the stupendous and cosmogonal philosophy of the Bhagwad Gita in comparison with which our modern world and its literature seems puny."

***

" Whenever I have read any part of the Vedas , I have felt that some unearthly and unknown light illuminated me . In the great teaching of the Vedas there is no touch of sectarianism . it is of all ages , climbs , and nationalists and is the royal road for the attainment of the great knowledge. When I read it , I feel that I am under the spangled heavens of a summer night. "

- **Henry David Thoreau** (1817-1862) An American philosopher , poet and  environmental scientist.

## 4 (19) ARTHUR SCHOPENHAUER

"And if, indeed, in addition to this he is a partaker of the benefit conferred by the Vedas, the access to which, opened to us through the Upanishads, is in my eyes the greatest advantage which this still young century enjoys over previous ones, because I believe that the influence of the Sanscrit literature will penetrate not less deeply than did the revival of Greek literature in the fifteenth century: if, I say, the reader has also already received and assimilated the sacred, primitive Indian wisdom, then is he best of all prepared to hear what I have to say to him. My work will not speak to him, as to many others, in a strange and even hostile tongue; for, if it does not sound too vain, I might express the opinion that each one of the individual and disconnected aphorisms which make up the Upanishads may be deduced as a consequence from the thought I am going to impart, though the converse, that my thought is to be found in the Upanishads, is by no means the case."

***

"The view of things ... that all plurality is only apparent, that in the endless series of individuals, passing simultaneously and successively into and out of life, generation after generation, age after age, there is but one and the same entity really existing, which is present and identical in all alike; — this theory ... may be carried back to the remotest antiquity. It is the alpha and omega of the oldest book in the world, the sacred Vedas, whose dogmatic part, or rather esoteric teaching, is found in the Upanishads. There, in almost every page this profound doctrine lies enshrined; with tireless repetition, in countless adaptations, by many varied parables and similes it is expounded and inculcated."

***

"Fromevery sentence (Of the Upanishads) deep,original and sublime thoughts arise and the whole is pervaded by a high and holy and earnestspirit. In the whole world there is no study so beneficial and so elevating as that of Upanishads. It has been the solace of my life – It will be the solace of my death. They are the product of the highest wisdom…"

***

"From every sentence (of the Upanishads) deep, original and sublime thoughts arise, and the whole is pervaded by a high and holy and earnest spirit…. They are destined sooner or later to become the faith of the people."

***

The Indian air surrounds us, the original thoughts of kindred spirits …

***

It IS the most profitable and most elevating reading which is possible in the world. [Sanskrit literature is] 'the greatest gift of our century.

***

Access to the Vedas is the greatest privilege this century may claim over all previous centuries. How entirely does the Upanishad breathe throughout the holy spirit of the Vedas! How is every one, who, by a diligent study of its Persian Latin has become familiar with that incomparable book, stirred by that spirit to the very depth of his Soul!


— **Arthur Schopenhauer** (1788-1860) German Philosopher .He is famous for his work "The World as Will and Representation".

## 4 (20) WILHELM VON HUMBOLDT


"Sanskrit is the unsurpassed zenith in the whole development of languages yet known to us."

***


"The most beautiful, perhaps the only true philosophical song( ShrimadBhagvad Gita ) existing in any known tongue.. perhaps the deepest and loftiest thing the world has to show "


- **Wilhelm Von Humbolt** (1767-1835)A Prussian philosopher, linguist, government functionary, diplomat, and founder of the Humboldt University of Berlin Prussian minister of education , a brilliant linguist and the founder of the science of general linguistics.

## 4 (21) VICTOR COUSIN

"When we read the poetical and philosophical monuments of the East- above all , those of India , which are beginning to spread in Europe — we discover their many a truth , and truths so profound , and which make such a contrast with the meanness of the results at which European genius has sometimes stopped . that we are constrained to bend the knee before the philosophy of the East, and to see in this cradle of the human race the native land of the highest philosophy "

**-Victor Cousin** (1792-1867) A French philosopher and founder of school of "eclecticism.

## 4 (22 ) HU SHIH

"India conquered and dominated china culturally for twenty centuries without ever having to send a single soldier across her border "

– **Hu Shih** (1891-1962) A Chinese diplomat,essayist, literary scholar, philosopher and politician.

## 4 (23) APOLLONIUS TYANAEUS

"In India I found a race of mortals living upon the Earth, but not adhering to it. Inhabitingcities .but not being fixed to them .possessing everything but possessed by nothing."

– **Apollonius Tyanaeus** (3 BC – 97 AD) AGreek Traveler and Philosopher.

## 4 (24) JAMES H. BILLINGTON

"If we were to study , there is so much that is unknown , I have been talking to people of millions of manuscripts that nobody has ever read of Indian History , India has got to take its own heritage more seriously ; not only preserve but bring it forth and make it intelligible ."

-**James H. Billington** (1929-2018)An American academic and author who taught history at harvard and princton University He served as the 13thLibrarian, of Congress of United states. Largest library of the world.

### 4 (25) LIN YUTANG

"India has as rich a culture, as creative an imagination and wit and humor as any china has to offer and that India was Chinas teacher in religion and imaginative literature and the worlds  in trigonometry, quadratic equation , grammar, phonetics , Arabian nights , animal fables , chess as well as philosophy and that she inspired Boccaccio, Goethe, Herder, Schopenhauer, Emerson and probably also old Aesop."

- **Lin Yutang** (1895-1976) A Chinese inventor, linguist, novelist, philosopher and translator.

### 4 (26) FRANCOIS –MARIE AROUET, VOLTAIRE

"I am convinced that everything has come down to us from the banks of the Ganges, astronomy, astrology, metempsychosis, etc. It does not behoove us, who were only savages and barbarians when these Indians and Chinese people's were civilized and learned, to dispute their antiquity."

- **Francois –Marie Arouet, Voltaire** (1694-1778) A French Enlightmentwriter , historian and philosopher famous for his wit and criticism .He was supporter of freedom of speech and freedom of religion.

# 4 (27) LEONARD BLOOMFIELD

"It was in India, however, that there rose a body of knowledge which was destined to revolutionize European ideas about language. Panini Grammar taught Europeans to analyze speech forms; when one compared the constituent parts, the resemblances, which hitherto had been vaguely recognized, could be set forth with certainty and precision."

-**Leonard Bloomfield**( 1887-1949) An American linguist He is considered to be the father of American distributionalism.

# 4 (28) FRANZ BOPP

"Sanskrit was at one time the only language of the world. It is more perfect and copious than Greek and Latin."

-**Franz Bopp**(1791-1867)A German Linguist known for extensive comparison work of Indo European languages .

# 4 (29) JOHN W DU BOIS

"Sanskrit is the origin of modern languages of Europe ."

- **John W Du Bois**, An American Professor of linguistics at University of California ,Santa Barbara.

# 4 (30) ARTHUR ANTHONY MACDONELL

"The intellectual debt of Europe to Sanskrit literature has been undeniably great. It may perhaps become greater still in the years that are to come. We (Europeans) are still behind the making even our alphabet a perfect one."

-**Arthur Anthony Macdonell**( 1854-1930) Was born in India to a British Army Soldier . was A noted Sanskrit scholar.

# 4 (31) VYASS HOUSTON

"The fact is that Sanskrit is more deeply interwoven into the fabric of the collective world consciousness than anyone perhaps knows. After many thousands of years, Sanskrit still lives with a vitality that can breathe life, restore unity and inspire peace on our tired and troubled planet. It is a sacred gift, an opportunity. The future could be very bright. ... In ancient India the intention to discover truth was so consuming, that in the process, they discovered perhaps the most perfect tool for fulfilling such a search that the world has ever known"

-**VyassHouston** , is the founder and director of the American Sanskrit Institute.

# 4 (32) GEORGES IFRAH

"Sanskrit means "complete", "perfect" and "definitive". In fact, this language is extremely elaborate, almost artificial, and is capable of describing multiple levels of meditation, states of consciousness and psychic, spiritual and even intellectual processes. As for vocabulary, its richness is considerable and highly diversified. Sanskrit has for centuries lent itself admirably to the diverse rules of prosody and versification. Thus we can see why poetry has played such a preponderant role in all of Indian culture and Sanskrit literature. "

- Georges Ifrah (1947-2019)teacher of mathematics, a French author and a self-taught historian of mathematics.

## 4 (33) FRIEDRICH VON SCHLEGEL

"There is no language in the world, even Greek, which has the clarity and the philosophical precision of Sanskrit. India is not only at the origin of everything she is superior in
everything, intellectually, religiously or politically and
even the Greek heritage seems pale in comparison."

-**Friedrich von Schlegel** (1772-1829) AGerman poet, literary critic, philosopher, philologist, and Indologist.

## 4 (34) SIR  MONIER MONIER-WILLIAMS

"India though it has more than five hundred spoken dialects, has only  one sacred  language and  only one  sacred literature,  accepted  and  revered  by  all adherence  of Hinduism alike,  however  diverse  in  race, dialect,  rank  and creed. That  language is Sanskrit  and Sanskrit  literature,  the  only  repository  of the Veda or knowledge in  its  widest  sense,  the  only vehicle  of Hindu  mythology, philosophy, law, the mirror in  which  all  the  creeds,  opinions, and customs and  usages  of  the Hindus are  faithfully reflected  and  the  only  quarry  whence  the  requisite materials  may  be  obtained  for  improving the vernaculars or  for  expressing important religious and scientific ideas."

"By Sanskrit is meant the learned language of India - the language  of  its cultured inhabitants,  the  language  of its religion, its literature and science - not by any means a dead  language,  but  one  still  spoken  and  written  by educated  men  by  all  parts  of  the  country, from Kashmir to Cape  Comorin, from Bombay to Calcutta and Madras."

**-Sir   MonierMonier-Williams** (1819-1899)ABritish scholar Professor of sanskrit at  Oxford University.

### 4 (35) VECENTE AVELINO

"India is the only country which has known God and if anyone wants to know God he must know India."
**-Vecente Avelino**, A Spanish scientist  Professor of Physics  at Universitat de València.

# 4 (36) ARTHUR LLEWELLYN BASHAM

"The ancient civilisation of India differs from those of Egypt, Mesopotamia and Greece, in that its traditions have been preserved without a break down to the present day. Until the advent of the archaeologist, the peasant of Egypt or Iraq had no knowledge of the culture of his forefathers, and it is doubtful whether his Greek counterpart had any but the vaguest ideas about the glory of Periclean Athens. In each case there had been an almost complete break with the past. On the other hand...to this day legends known to the humblest Indian recall the names of shadowy chieftains who lived nearly a thousand years before."

**-Arthur Llewellyn Basham** ( 1914 – 1986) A noted historian, Indologist.

# 4 (37) ANNIE BESANTNÉE

"India is the mother of religion. In her are combined science and religion in perfect harmony, and that is the Hindu religion, and it is India that shall be again the spiritual mother of the world."

**-Annie Besantnee** ( 1847 – 1933) A British Socialist and theosophists .

## 4 (38) KEITH BARRY CRITCHLOW

"I learned that Bharat is the most ancient source of living wisdom (spirituality) and that it has always generated its revelations world wide."

-**Keith Barry Critchlow** (1933-2020) A British artist, lecturer, author, Sacred Geometer, professor of architecture.

## 4 (39) FRANK DIXON

"India has many strengths which make it one of the greatest countries in the world. I believe India's greatest strength is the Indian people, in particular their spiritual devotion and purity. Many Indians see beyond illusion and understand the deeper meaning is best displayed by the custom of bowing of life. Perhaps this to the God within when greeting another person. Many Western people visit India to find spiritual inspiration, clarity and renewal. This focus on the deeper reality of humanity's oneness with nature and each other is needed to address growing environmental and social problems around the world. The Indian people model the peace, wisdom, love and respect needed to achieve the beautiful, prosperous, sustainable world that all humanity seeks."

- **Frank Dixon** (1920-2008) A former Director — Research, Innovest Venture Partners.

# 4 (40) HERMANN KARL HESSE

"India is not only a country and something geographical, but the home and the youth of the soul, the everywhere and nowhere, the oneness of all times."

- Hermann Karl Hesse ( 1877 –  1962) A German-Swiss poet, novelist, and painter.

# 4 (41) CARL GUSTAV JUNG

"Great and enduring civilizations like those of the Hindus and the Chinese were built upon this foundation and developed from it a discipline of self-knowledge which they brought to a high pitch of refinement both in philosophy and practice."

***

"As we study the philosophy of the Upanishads, the impression grows on us that the attainment of this path is not exactly the simplest of tasks. Our Western superciliousness in the face of these Indian insights is a mark of our barbarian nature, which has not the remotest inkling of their extraordinary depth and astonishing psychological accuracy."

-Carl  Gustav  Jung (   1875 –   1961)  A Swiss psychiatrist and psychoanalyst who
founded analytical psychology.

# 4 (42) RABINDRANATH TAGORE

"What India has been, the whole world is now. The whole world is becoming one country through scientific facility. And the moment is arriving when you also must find a basis of unity which is not political. If India can offer to the world her solution, it will be a contribution to humanity. There is only one history — the history of Man. All national histories are merely chapters in the larger one."

-Rabindranath Tagore ( 1861– 1941) A Bengali polymath who worked as a poet, writer, playwright, composer, philosopher, social reformer and painter.

# 4 (43) HERBERT GEORGE WELLS

"The history of India for many centuries had been happier, less fierce, and more dreamlike than any other history. In these favorable conditions, they built a character meditative and peaceful and a nation of philosophers such as could have existed except nowhere in India."

-Herbert George Wells (1866 –1946) An English writer.

### 4 (44) HSUAN TSANG

"The ordinary people ... are upright and honourable... They are faithful to their oaths and promises... In their behavior there is much gentleness and sweetness."

***

"They do not practice deceit, and they keep their sworn obligations. . . . They will not take anything wrongfully, and they yield more than fairness requires."

**-HsuanTsang**(Xuanzang) ( 602 – 664)A 7th-century Chinese Buddhist monk, scholar, traveler, and translator.

### 4 (45) LEE KUAN YEW

"India is a nation of unfulfilled greatness. Its potential has lain fallow, under used."

**-Lee Kuan Yew** ( 1923 – 2015)A Singaporean barrister and statesman who served as the first prime minister of Singapore.

### 4 (46) MAHARSHI ARVIND

"For what is a nation? What is our mother-country? It is not a piece of earth, nor a figure of speech, nor a fiction of the mind. It is a mighty Shakti, composed of the Shaktis of all the millions of units that make up the nation, just as Bhawani Mahisha Mardini sprang into being from the Shaktis of all the millions of gods assembled in one mass of force and welded into unity. The Shakti we call India, Bhawani Bharati, is the living unity of the Shaktis of three hundred million people."

***

"Spirituality is the master key of the Indian mind. It is this dominant inclination of India which gives character to all the expressions of her culture. In fact, they have grown out of her inborn spiritual tendency of which her religion is a natural out flowering. The Indian mind has always realized that the Supreme is the Infinite and perceived that to the soul in Nature the Infinite must always present itself in an infinite variety of aspects. The aggressive and quite illogical idea of a single religion for all mankind, a religion universal by the very force of its narrowness, one set of dogmas, one cult, one system of ceremonies, one ecclesiastical ordinance, one array of prohibitions and injunctions which all minds must accept on peril of persecution by men and spiritual rejection or eternal punishment by God, that grotesque creation of humane unreason which has been the parent of so much intolerance, cruelty and obscurantism and aggressive fanaticism, has never been able to take firm hold of the Indian mentality."

***

"Indian religion has always felt that since the minds, the temperaments and the intellectual affinities of men are unlimited in their variety, a perfect liberty of thought and of worship must be allowed to the individual in his approach to the Infinite."

**-Aurobindo Ghose -Maharshi Arvind** (1872-1950)  An Indian Philosopher , Yogi, Maharshi, Poet and Indian Nationalist. He was also a journalist , editing newspapers such as vandemataram . He joined the Indian movement for independence .

## 4 (47) KEITH BELLOW

"There are some parts of the world that, once visited, get into your heart and won't go. For me, India is such a place. When I first visited, I was stunned by the richness of the land, by its lush beauty and exotic architecture, by its ability to overload the senses with the pure, concentrated intensity of its colours, smells, tastes, and sounds. It was as if all my life I had been seeing the world in black and white and, when brought face-to-face with India, experienced everything re-rendered in brilliant technicolour."

— **Keith Bellows**(1951-2015)**An** Editor in chief of National Geographic Traveller and Vice-President of National Geographic SocietyOf America.

## 4 (48) CARL SAGAN

"The Hindu Religion is the only one of the world's great faiths dedicated to the idea that the cosmos itself undergoes an immense indeed an innate , number of deaths and revirths, It is the only religion in which the time sacales  correspond to , to those of modern scientific cosmology , its cycle runs from our ordinary day and night to a day and night of Brahma , 8.64 billion years long . longer than the  age of  the earth  or the sun and about half the time scale the Big Bang. And there are much longer time scale still ."

***

"The most elegant and sublime of these is a representation of the creation of the universe at the beginning  of each cosmic cycle , a motif  known as the cosmic dance of shiva . The God  Called in this manifest nataraja , the Dance king In the upper right hand is a drum whose sound is sound of creation , in the upper left hand is a tongue of flame , a reminder that the universe, newly created , with billion of years from now will be utterly destroyed ."

**-Carl Sagan** (1934-1996) An American astronomer, Planetary scientist, cosmologist, astrophysicist, science communicator , author and professor .

### 4 (49) JULIUS ROBERT OPPENHEIMER

"Access to the Vedas is the greatest privilege this century may claim over all previous centuries."

***

"The general notions about human understanding... which are illustrated by discoveries in atomic physics are not in the nature of things wholly unfamiliar, wholly unheard of or new. Even in our own culture they have a history, and in Buddhist and Hindu thought a more considerable and central place. What we shall find [in modern physics] is an exemplification, an encouragement, and a refinement of old wisdom."

***

"The juxtaposition of Western civilization's most terrifying scientific achievement with the most dazzling description of the mystical experience given to us by the Bhagavad Gita, India's greatest literary monument."

***

"When on July 16 1945 RobertOpenheimer observed first atomic explosion he recited following verses from SrimadBhagawad Gita

divi sūryasahasrasyabhavedyugapadutthitā

yadibhāḥsadṛśīsāsyādbhāsastasyamahātmanaḥ(11-

12).

"If the radiance of a thousand suns were to burst at once into the sky, that would be like the splendor of the mighty one".

181

"kālo'smilokakṣayakṛtpravṛddholokānsamāhartumihapr

avṛttaḥ"(11-32).

which he translated as "I am become Death, the destroyer of worlds."

 In 1965, when he was persuaded to quote again for a television broadcast, he said:

We knew the world would not be the same. A few people laughed, a few people cried. Most people were silent. I remembered the line from the Hindu scripture, the Bhagavad Gita; Vishnu is trying to persuade the Prince that he should do his duty and, to impress him, takes on his multi-armed form and says, "Now I am become Death, the destroyer of worlds." I suppose we all thought that, one way or another. "

**-Julius Robert Oppenheimer** (1904-1967) Scientist, philosopher, bohemian, and radical. A theoretical physicist and the Supervising Scientist for the Manhattan Project .

### 4 (50) OCTOVIO PAZ

"The Hindu genius is a love for abstraction and, at the same time, a passion for the concrete image. At times it is rich, at others prolix. It has created the most lucid and the most instinctive art. It is abstract and realistic, sexual and intellectual, pedantic and sublime. It lives between extremes, it embraces the extremes, rooted in the earth and drawn to an invisible beyond."

**-Octavio Paz (1914-1998) A** Mexican poet and diplomat. For his body of work, he was awarded the 1977 Jerusalem Prize, the 1981 Miguel de Cervantes

Prize, the 1982 Neustadt International Prize for Literature, and the 1990 Nobel Prize in Literature.

## 4 (51) GEOREGE BERBARD SHAW

"The Indian way of life provides the vision of the natural, real way of life. We veil ourselves with unnatural masks. On the face of India are the tender expressions which carry the mark of the Creators hand."

***

"The apparent multiplication of gods is bewildering at the first glance, but you soon discover that they are the same GOD. There is always one uttermost God who defies personification. This makes Hinduism the most tolerant religion in the world, because its one transcendent God includes all possible gods. In fact Hinduism is so elastic and so subtle that the most profound Methodist, and crudest idolater, are equally at home with it."

**-George Bernard Shaw** (1856-1950) known at his insistence as Bernard Shaw, was an Irish playwright, critic, polemicist and political activist.a vegetarian and Nobel Laureate in Literature.

## 4 (52) SRI MADHUKARNATH

"The Upanishads represent the high watermark not only of Hindu philosophy but of spiritual literature anywhere in the world. These marvellous discourses and dialogues between self- realised seers, known as Rishis, and one or more disciples, contain powerful and eloquent statements regarding the ultimate reality in its multifarious facets. They have been well described as providing an "ecstatic slide show of reality, a privileged glimpse of the unitive vision in which all thing are one in a world aflame with God". They contain some of the most eloquent passages, such as "I have seen that Great Being shining like a thousand suns beyond the darkness; it is only by knowing that Being that we can achieve immortality."

-**Sri Madhkarnath** – also known as Sri M ( Born as Mumtz Ali -1949) Indian Yogi, Spiritual Guide , Social reformer and educationalist.

## 4 (53) MICHAEL N. NAGLER

"Since the discovery of the Upanishads by the West, not a few Westerners have gone to them as a source of the "perennial philosophy," a fascinating witness to an ancient civilization and its unique religious system; others, like Yeats, have been drawn by their poetic beauty. But the first Western philosopher to stumble on them, Arthur Schopenhauer, was looking for much, much more. And they did not disappoint him."

"At no time has the "Upanishadic" vision of a Heraclitus or an Augustine really become our own (of the West). Here the Upanishads may today challenge us (Westerners) very deeply to put in place fundamentally different concepts of who we are, and to build a life of thoughts, of personal habits, of lifestyles, of relationships, of institutions and values and finally even of foreign policy, based on the unity of consciousness rather than on the separateness and competitiveness of biological fragments."

-**Michael N. Nagler**, is professor emeritus of Classics and Comparative Literature at UC Berkeley.

## 4 (54) WALT WHITMAN

"These (Upanisads) are really the thoughts of all men in all ages and lands; they are not original with me. If they are not yours as much as mine, they are nothing or next to nothing."

-**Walt Whitman** (Walter Whitman Jr. (1819 – 1892) was an American poet, essayist, and journalist.

## 4 (55) PAUL JAKOB DEUSSEN

"On the tree of wisdom there is no fairer flower than the Upanishads, and no finer fruit than the Vedanta philosophy."

- **Paul Jakob Deussen** ( 1845 – 1919) A German Indologist and professor of philosophy at University of Kiel.

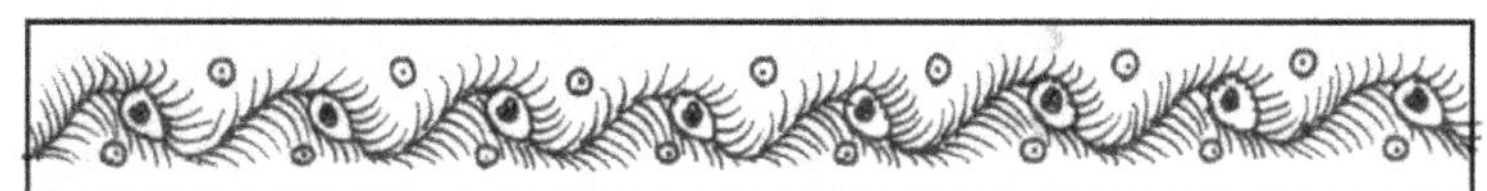

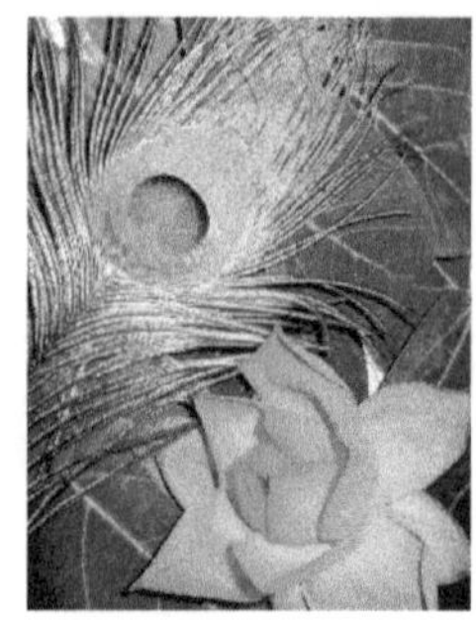

* * * * * *

वंदे मातरम …

VANDE MATARAM …

भारत माता की जय …

BHARAT MATA KI JAI …

जय हिंद …

JAI HIND …

# REFERENCES

(1) Lin Yu Tang, " Wisdom Of India " (2005) Jaico Publishing House

(2) Swami Vivekanand  " Compete works of swami Vivekanand" (Vol I to IX ) (2016) Advaita Ashram , Kolkata

(3) Dr. Ravindra Kumar " Nationalism in the Vedas " Article published on Monday 8 th August 2022 in Business Economics https://businesseconomics.in/nationalism-vedas

(4) Joshua J. Mark " The Edicts of Ashoka the Great" Published on 29 th June 2020 In World History Encyclopedia

https://www.worldhistory.org/Edicts_of_Ashoka/

(5) "Inscriptions in Parliament House " May 2014, Published by " Lok sabha Secretariat "

https://loksabhadocs.nic.in/our%20parliament/Increptions%20 in%20parliament%20house.pdf

(6) Sidharth Bhatia " India Discovers herself again "The full text of Jawaharlal Nehru's " Tryst With destiny speech" Published on 28 th August 2022 in janata Weekly

https://janataweekly.org/india-discovers-herself-again-the-full-text-of-jawaharlal-nehrus-tryst-with-destiny-speech/

(7) https://www.wikipedia.org/

(8) https://en.wikiquote.org/wiki/Main_Page

(9) https://www.brainyquote.com/

(10) https://www.goodreads.com/quotes

(11) https://www.azquotes.com/

(12) https://ndkul.blogspot.com/2017/10/blog-post_68.html

For sangyanSukt of Rigveda

(13) https://nios.ac.in/media/documents/bgp/Secondary_Hindi/Veda_Adhyayan_245/245_book1/245_Book1_L8.pdf

For sangyanSukt of Rigveda

(14) https://www.taleof2backpackers.com/quotes-about-india/

For quotations on influence of India

(15) https://www.insightsonindia.com/2008/04/22/quotes-on-india/

For quotations on influence of India

(16) https://www.pgurus.com/6-famous-international-physicists-who-were-influenced-by-hindu-dharma/

Famous Scientists on hinduisam

(17)https://pragyata.com/a-look-at-india-from-the-views-of-other-scholars/

Various western scholars on India
(18)http://www.onlinedarshan.com/minds-on-hinduism/index.htm

Great minds on India

(19)https://www.caclubindia.com/forum/if-you-are-an-indian-read-this--212190.asp

For quotations on India

(20)https://www.hinduismfacts.org/hinduism-quotes/

Quotes on Hinduisam

(21)http://thehinduforum.com/index.php?threads/quotes-by-famous-personalities-on-hinduism-and-india.502/

Quotes on Hinduisam

(22)https://www.india.gov.in/india-glance/national-symbols#:~:text=National%20Flag&text=In%20the%20centre%20of%20the,and%20auspiciousness%20of%20the%20land.

National Symbols of India
(23)https://upanishads.org.in/quotes/others

Quotations on Upanishads

(24)https://www.boloji.com/articles/717/influence-of-upanishads-in-the-west       -       Influence of Upanishad on west .

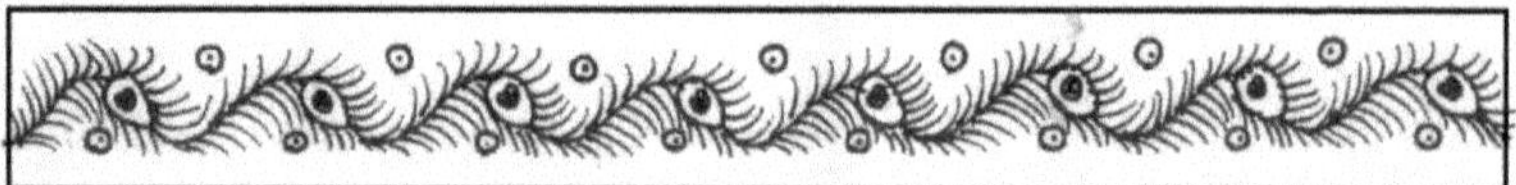